C000066030

The demands of ministry ... experiences of ministry has ... thing as a "normal week". W. ... . *management* can be very helpful it also holds the danger of enabling us to become more efficient in our busyness. What is required is the practice of time *wisdom*. Stephen has done us all a service by sharing his wisdom, by encouraging us not simply to reflect on our busyness but to also have a go at changing our lives. His questions and challenges are a gift to any busy minister.

DR TIM LING

National Adviser for Continuing Ministerial Development, Church of England

Stephen Cherry uses his own experience of getting the best from a busy life to create this accessible and challenging book. Enriched with quotation and story which build collective wisdom, it takes us into a new way of understanding how to control our time in a way which will enable personal and spiritual development.

CANON MALCOLM GRUNDY

Founding Director of the Foundation for Church Leadership

Beyond Busyness abounds with practical wisdom for those engaged in Christian Ministry. At a time when busyness, anxiety and stress characterise the lives of many of the Church's ministers, Stephen Cherry has written a much-needed book. It very effectively challenges ministers to reflect on how they approach and use the gift of time. Each of the short 28 sessions offers considerable insight into the nature of time and encourages ministers to confront their current habits and develop new life-giving practices through which their ministry can thrive and they can flourish. Every minister should spend time not only reading *Beyond Busyness* but integrating its wisdom into their lives.

DR JOCELYN BRYAN

Director of Postgraduate Studies, St John's College, Durham University

Beyond Busyness

Time Wisdom for Ministry

STEPHEN CHERRY

Sacristy Press
PO Box 612, Durham, DH1 9HT

www.sacristy.co.uk

First published in 2012 by Sacristy Press, Durham

Sacristy Limited, registered in England & Wales, number 7565667

British Library Cataloguing-in-Publication Data
A catalogue record for the book is available from the British Library

ISBN 978-1-908381-05-7

O remember how short my time is

PSALM 89.46, COVERDALE PSALTER

Nine tenths of wisdom is being wise in time.

THEODORE ROOSEVELT[1]

Contents

Introducing Time Wisdom

Having been a parish priest for twelve years (and before that a college chaplain) I was appointed to a complex diocesan and cathedral portfolio. As I looked forward to the role it became clear that I would need to be very careful with my diary. My predecessor had been full-time, but I had to do his job in addition to making 25% of my time available for the Cathedral. The role also involved being in three places: my diocesan office, my study at home, and in and around the Cathedral. It would be very easy, I thought, to spend a lot of time travelling between the three, with or without the relevant papers, for the next meeting or encounter. Shortly after I arrived, a colleague left and I had to take on responsibility for the Continuing Ministerial Development for all clergy other than curates and training incumbents. A few years later this expanded to include the same role for the Readers of the diocese. For two years I was also seconded to a project development role to establish a Regional Training Partnership for Adult Learning and Theological Education. Most recently, and just as I was completing this book, I was seconded to work on a Cathedral development project, leaving me to do the diocesan role in about two days per week.

The story is obviously personal but the underlying plot will be shockingly familiar to many in ministry today—take one person and keep giving them more and more to do. For some it will be more parishes, for others it will be extra roles and responsibilities. And none of these additional roles or parishes are ever any easier than the existing ones. The actual work and challenge of ministry seems to get harder and harder all the time. The system is creaking and people are cracking as more is continuously expected of them. Another book might discuss the reasons; however, this book is not about cause or effect, but rather living with the consequences. It is about how to survive, and possibly even thrive, in a Church where there is far more to be done than can possibly be done. It is a sad truth that familiar methods of ministry are no longer practical and accustomed priorities have to be renegotiated.

This book is about time and its apparent shortage, except that the book is *not* based on the widespread belief that time is too short or that people are being asked to do the impossible. It *is* based on the conviction that there is plenty of time and that what will be called here "time wisdom" is a frame of mind, a set of attitudes, beliefs and practices that will allow people to be good and faithful ministers, possibly even successful ones, in the circumstances which are already upon us and which are continually increasing.

As my ministry moved into the zone of serious overload I was fortunate in many ways to have Continuing Ministerial Development (CMD) as one of my responsibilities. It focused my attention on the pressures that other clergy face, but gave a positive framework for doing so. It quickly became clear to me that "time" was a major and critical issue for many clergy and it seemed to me that as CMD officer I should try to do something about it. I turned to the material available on time management and began to explore the advice that is given. It was a fruitful exploration and I remain interested in all the tips, techniques, skills and habits which come under this heading. Yet, I also began to realise that "time management" did not quite hit the spot for clergy, especially those in parish ministry or other contexts where there were multiple layers of not-very-clearly-articulated expectation, uneven levels of demand, a high degree of autonomy and where unplanned eventualities could suddenly demand time and attention.

In 2009 I devised and led a clergy conference on the theme "Time Matters". We looked at time from a range of perspectives including a lecture on the physics of time and another on ageing. Our bishop presented some new research and gave us a Bible Study on "the Sabbath".[2] We got someone along to talk about nostalgia—what it is and how it impacts on ministry—and we reflected on how the liturgical calendar structured and shaped our lives. We did a little bit of work on managing time, but again, it did not really seem to fit. A number of clergy who had been in other professions before ordination said to me that they used to be good at time management but found that in parish ministry it was much more difficult. I could see the point, though I could not quite articulate why ministry and time management don't really go together as well as we hope they should.

After the conference, I began to put together some resources to help clergy not only manage their time but understand something of its human, spiritual and theological significance and richness. It was out of this work that the idea of "time wisdom" was born. I produced a small booklet called "Time Wisdom for Ministry" which was appreciated by clergy in Durham diocese and used by trainers further afield.

Beyond Busyness is a development of that resource. It is another step on the journey of trying to connect the reality and experience of time with the demands and realities of ministry today. The idea is to present the basic elements of a time wisdom that will be good enough for those in ministry. Everyone has some time wisdom and we all have the opportunity to develop more or better time wisdom.

My hopes are that this book will help ministers develop a time wisdom which will assist them in navigating the very considerable pressures that they face today, and that as they do so they will not only discover that they can survive but also begin to flourish and thrive. A Church in mission needs its public representatives to be credible witnesses to the whole Christian gospel. That always involves personal faith, pastoral sensitivity, sincere care, and palpable prayerfulness but also effective administration, competent management and perhaps above all else a relaxed acceptance of the pressures and strains which bear witness to a life being lived by trust and hope. What a Church in mission, and under pressure, does not need is people who come across as constantly hassled, anxious or busy. Of course we all have days like that. But we need to learn from them, not get used to them. We need not only to be careful with regard to our diaries, but wise about time.

Since first noted down by Joseph Licklider in 1965 it has almost become a truism to note that "people tend to overestimate what can be done in one year and to underestimate what can be done in five or ten years." The idea easily transfers to ministry, and so too do some of the practices and habits of effective executives. Yet being a church leader, a minister of the gospel, is not the same as being an executive. It has different priorities and is based on different values and is lived in different rhythms. Christian ministry fits into time in a different way to any other kind of work. It is for this reason that time management books, programmes and courses often do not quite work as intended as far as clergy are concerned.

It is also the reason why good, effective people who have been exemplary and efficient professionals in other areas sometimes struggle with the transfer to full-time ministry. The pressures on ministers and church leaders are subtle. They can sometimes be insidious. The old saying is that "the devil makes work for idle hands" but a more profound point might be that some spiritual force or other is constantly making sure that the hands and minds that should be set aside for the work of the gospel get tied up in lesser matters. All of which means that the medicine needed to cure ministerial busyness is a little stronger and more sophisticated than the tips, techniques and methods of time management.

This is where time wisdom comes in.

Time wisdom is the combination of skills, habits and spirituality that lies behind effective ministry over a long period of time. In order to be an effective and good minister, to survive and thrive in church leadership, it is essential to build up good time wisdom. As such, time wisdom is the antidote to the disease of busyness.

How to Use this Book

It is up to you, of course, but here are some suggestions.

This book is made up of twenty-eight sessions, so one way of approaching it might be to do a session a day for four weeks. Equally, you might like to do a session a week for just over six months. On the other hand, you could just spend a day, or two half days, going through it all.

The twenty-eight sessions are grouped together in six parts. Each part covers some related themes and all bar the final one conclude with an "interlude". This is an opportunity to stand back and attend to the mystery and spirituality of time. It really is a big subject and it has puzzled very many wise people and boggled some of the greatest minds. Together these interludes point to the multidimensional and holistic nature of time. This is something to which time management does not always attend, but it is integral to time wisdom.

Each of the twenty-eight sessions has the same format. There is a micro-essay on the topic, theme or phenomenon connected with time. Then there are a few questions to encourage you to think through some aspects of it. Each session also has a short quotation called "Food for Thought" about time and it ends with a positive practical suggestion, a "Why Not". "Food for Thought" and "Why Not" are not precisely or necessarily derived from the main content of the session. Some are rather lateral ideas and some connect up with content of earlier and later sessions. This structure reflects the reality that time wisdom is not a coherent or linear body of knowledge that can be "applied" but a more or less adequate and interconnected set of insights, habits and practices.

At the very end of the book comes the Postlude. In this short essay, various ideas and insights are drawn together to help give substance to one of the main features of time wisdom, a sense of "timescape".

It is not always easy to learn from a written resource. Before starting on Session 1, read though the list of "problems" and "suggestions" below to see if that suggests any ways in which you might best make use of the sessions to grow in time wisdom.

| **Problem:** | **With the best will in the world I find that my mind wanders whenever I try to read books like this.** |
| Suggestion: | If you find anything boring stop reading it immediately and move to the next section. |

Problem: **I have attended time management courses and they just don't work for me in ministry.**

Suggestion: I'm not surprised. That's why the idea here is not time *management* but time *wisdom*. The differences are summarised in Session 7.

Problem: **Some people (and I am one of them) don't learn by reading and writing.**

Suggestion: The actual amount of reading required per session is very small. When it comes to the questions for reflection, if you prefer not to write answers do something else. Draw a picture. Chat to the wall. Talk to a recording device. Phone a friend and tell them what you are thinking.

Problem: **Whenever I come across anything about management or leadership in the Church it seems to come from another world: business, industry, or even the military. It's usually not that relevant and is invariably without a hint of theology.**

Suggestion: I do draw on some "secular" time management ideas, but very selectively. *Beyond Busyness* is based on lived experience of ministry and careful analysis of the reality of ministerial life. There is not a lot of theology on the page, but there is a lot of theology behind the page and between the lines.

Problem: **I don't like working on my own.**

Suggestion: Then don't. Persuade a colleague to work with you through the book, or do it as a cell group or Chapter. In the latter case it might be advisable to do, say, four sessions together (at successive meetings—allocate about 15 minutes) but the others either as individuals or in pairs.

Problem: **I am too busy to spend my time on things like this.**

Suggestion: No you're not. Go straight to Session 3 to find out why.

The best way to learn is often to teach (which is maybe why I have taken the trouble to prepare this resource while under what feels like real time pressure from too many jobs, roles, responsibilities . . .) How can you become a teacher of time wisdom to others? Might you be a campaigner for a "busy-free ministry" or even a "busy-free life"? It's an impossible dream, of course. There will always be busy days, but busy days can be positive responses to unexpected combinations of demands. Busy weeks, months and years—and busy people—well that's quite another issue. Busy ministers? Hopefully you will come to appreciate why that is an oxymoron. Even more hopefully, you will see it also becoming much rarer, not because the demands are fewer but because your wisdom is greater and your timescape more richly developed.

PART 1
Getting Started

The first three sessions set the scene and introduce the concept of "time wisdom". We consider the needs of busy ministers and take a look at some major "time traps" that are best avoided.

“ Time wisdom is attentive to the needs of the past, the future and the present. ”

SESSION 1
Your Hopes

It was a grim winter's day as about a dozen or so clergy gathered in a Church Hall in Jarrow. Parking had been a nightmare as a funeral was about to start in the church next door. We were all there with a purpose, to spend half a day together working on questions of time and ministry. They were ready to be told, but I was not yet ready to speak. I thought it better, first, to find out what they were hoping for out of the day and what their issues were with time. Why, after all, give time to the question of time?

So, I asked them what they were hoping for, what their needs were. And as they shared them so I scrawled their ideas on the ever-so-slightly damp flip chart paper with a pen that was on the verge of drying out. (It is, by the way, not a bad combination.) Here is the list:

1. Aware of not having enough of it.
2. The need to fit more into each day.
3. Want to make the best use of my time.
4. Aware of acting in two times—God's and ours.
5. How to marry two ministries together—determining priorities.
6. "I want a guilt-free day off!"
7. Help needed in making difficult decisions—both big ones and little ones.
8. How to say "no" to people when you don't really want to (but know you have to say "no" to someone sooner or later).
9. How to make the important, important—not just rushing to the urgent.
10. Addressing the knowing-doing gap in time management.
11. How to avoid conflict between types of ministry.
12. Planning.
13. Getting out of reactive mode.
14. Relating to time as a resource rather than as a master.
15. Keeping space in the diary for my refreshment.
16. Why do we need to please people and meet all their expectations?

It is a good list; varied, and, I think, typical. Some of the items are about the problem as it presents—for example, not enough time, failing to get a "guilt-free" day off, not always rushing to the next urgent thing, keeping space for refreshment in the diary. Others are a bit more technical—facing the competing demands of having more than one ministry, for instance. Others were about things like saying "no", making appropriate decisions, and resisting inappropriate expectations. This is a broad range of issues and points very helpfully to the whole spectrum of matters relevant to time wisdom. It's certainly enough to get us going in pursuit of adequate time wisdom to enable us flourish in ministry today.

Time for Reflection

◆ Which of the 16 points is closest to what you might have said if you had been at the workshop?
◆ Are there any others that particularly speak to you? Choose up to three.
◆ What might you have said if you have been there?

Food for Thought

Time is about God and the universe and all things human. Time is everywhere and it permeates everything: the cosmos, our solar system, the earth's past, present and future, sociological existence. As such it has suffused knowledge since the dawn of humanity. It has occupied such a central place in the history of ideas and cultural practice because the temporality of being confronts us with the immemorial, existential issues of life and death, origin and destiny. What then is time? We know that the clock tells us *the* time, but it not tell us what time *is*. We live time, we experience it daily as an integral part of existence. We know it intimately and yet the answer to this simple question seems extraordinarily difficult.[3]

Why Not . . . ?

There are lots of songs about time. Not as many "time songs" as "love songs" perhaps, but still many more than "money songs". Can you think of ten? Here are two to start you off: "Time After Time", "Yesterday".

Time Traps for Clergy

One of the bestselling time management books is called *The Time Trap*[4].
In the first edition the author Alec Mackenzie listed twenty time traps that
prevented people in business and technology achieving their goals. In the
fourth edition a new writer, Pat Nickerson, has revised the list on the basis
of recent research. Here are the top five items in the more recent edition.

1. Management by Crisis (this was top in the original list too)
2. Inadequate Planning (moved up from third place and incorporated
    "lack of self discipline" which was previously eighth)
3. Inability to say "no" (formerly ninth)
4. Poor Communication (a big rise from seventeenth)
5. Poorly Run Meetings (this was twelfth)

One of the most surprising things about this is that poor communication
has risen such a long way up the table over a period where the amount of
technological support for communicating has risen exponentially. The
problem, it would seem, is not with the gadgets but with the people using
them. There must be more to communicating clearly than sending many
emails or texts or tweets or building a website or writing a blog or carrying
around enough processing capacity to run a large international business or
medium sized country.

The problem is not our lack of technology, but our lack of skill and
wisdom.

However, poor communication is not the number one issue. At the top
of the list comes "management by crisis". This, I think translates in clergy
speak into the "busy me" syndrome. Management by crisis means that we
don't have time to do this (whatever it is) properly. We don't have time to
plan it carefully. We don't have time to identify the risks. We don't have time
to form a project team, delegate responsibility or clarify roles.

Management by crisis is not crisis management. That's a legitimate and
important responsibility for leaders as and when crises come about, and
they always will. Management by crisis is more a state of mind which either
believes that there must be crisis before action is required or which goes
about creating a sense of crisis to get others motivated.

Management by crisis creates the second trap—inadequate planning. Yet
it is itself perhaps created by trap number three, the inability to say "no". In

fact, if asked to identify the root problem this is where I would go. It is only the person who can say "no" who can say "yes" with sincerity. It is when we say "no" that we cash in our freedom and autonomy which are the basis of the value of our actions when we say "yes". You should never say "never", but you should, when necessary, say "no".

The mediaeval theologians were convinced that the root sin is pride. If they were right, and the root time problem is the inability to say "no", then might there be a connection between pride and the failure to say "no"? I think there may. The pride being shown in the arrogance which says, "Yes, of course I can do anything." The humble truth is that you can't and the sooner you realise that the better for you and for everyone else.

Time for Reflection

+ Which one of the top five time traps are you most likely to fall into?
+ When did you last say "no"?

Food for Thought

Why are deadlines so powerful? Why do they motivate us when everything else fails? Why do we let them distort our priorities?

The word "deadline" has its origins in military prisons. It is the point beyond which the prisoner would not be allowed to run while escaping. When they crossed the "deadline" escaping prisoners would be shot.

Maybe this explains why we find deadlines so terrifying and yet exhilarating. They combine the prospect of liberation with the fear of sudden death.

Why Not . . . ?

Write your own list of "time traps" for clergy and discuss it with some colleagues.

SESSION 3
Time Management and Time Wisdom

We often face the problem that there does not seem to be enough time to do everything that needs to be done. The answer to the problem that is often given is called "time management". For many in ministry, however, traditional time management does not quite work. Something more subtle is needed which takes into account some of the unpredictability of life and the spirituality of time. This time wisdom is connected to emotional intelligence as it also involves a degree of self-awareness. Different people relate to time differently and a time-wise approach involves knowing something about how the relationship between you, the clock and the calendar is different to your colleagues'.

The table in Figure 1 summarises some of the more significant differences between time management and time wisdom.

In a book about "Time Mastery", which is a similar idea to time wisdom, the authors suggest that whereas Time Management is the BA programme, what leaders in business need is a graduate course. I don't think it is a matter of academic level, as this might imply, but of the complexity of life—or work, or ministry. Traditional time management works best for people whose priorities can be identified in advance, weighed against each other, and then worked on in a way that is reasonably uninterrupted by unexpected events. Time wisdom is an approach for people living in a less predictable environment, in a situation where it is important to be responsive to events and opportunities as they arise. However, the context of ministry today is far from being leisure interrupted by occasional pastoral responses. There are many things to do and there is a need to make a difference, often through engaging in projects: all of which require time management skills. However, these skills must be placed in a broader framework which admits higher priorities. Time wisdom is the approach to time of those who know that it is often the interruptions which are the most important and significant challenges and tasks, but who nonetheless do have to get quite a lot done.

TIME MANAGEMENT	TIME WISDOM
Focus on developing skills and habits.	Focus on developing wisdom and character.
Focus on *chronos*—ongoing time.	Equally concerned with issues of *kairos* (the moment of opportunity) and matters of timing more generally.
Applies particularly to planning of tasks in relation to deadlines.	Applies to the realisation of high aspirations in complex environments.
Applies to the "work" environment.	Applies to the whole of life.
Based on the clock and calendar.	Based on the reality that the clock and calendar are only part of the story of "telling the time".
Focus on doing more in less time—quantitative.	Focus on doing the most important things as well as possible—qualitative.
Tends to involve convergent and analytical thought.	More open to imaginative and divergent thought.
Focus on self—what I can get done.	Focus on the wider community or team—how can we make the biggest difference.
Depends on strong boundaries and clear processes.	Sees boundaries and processes as a means to ends and so subject to transgression in the interests of higher aims.
Suspicious of multi-tasking.	Sees multi-tasking as normal.
Seeks to eliminate procrastination.	Emphasizes the importance of getting the timing right, recognizing that this will sometimes mean engaging in what looks like procrastination.
Sees time as limited, a scarce resource.	Sees time as both plentiful and relative.
Has no theology or spirituality of time.	Encourages a rich theology and spirituality of time and its stewardship.
Seeks to organize things so that the best use is made of the passing moments of present tense.	Is attentive to the demands and needs of the past, the future and the present.

Figure 1: Table summarising the differences between Time Management and Time Wisdom

Time for Reflection

- ◆ Which three rows in the table above seem to you to be the most significant and important?
- ◆ Are there some aspects of ministerial life in which time management works perfectly well?

Food for Thought

A preacher from Tanzania, having been told not to preach too lengthy a sermon, teased the congregation. "I know you English people often look at the clock, or your wristwatches. But we Africans look on the sun."

Why Not . . . ?

Do without your watch for a while—maybe when on holiday—and see how that changes your sense of time?

A Litany for Time Wisdom in Ministry

Response: Lord of the day
We give you our time.

That we might apply ourselves to work we have planned
and be open to unexpected calls on our time.

Lord of the day
We give you our time.

That we might exercise responsibility with care and
remain calm when challenged, threatened or rushed.

Lord of the day
We give you our time.

That we might appreciate the efforts of others,
even when they disappoint us.

Lord of the day
We give you our time.

That we might be good colleagues, collaborators and
partners to all with whom we share priorities.

Lord of the day
We give you our time.

That we might grow in our sense of vocation and help
others to open themselves to your call in their daily lives.

Lord of the day
We give you our time.

That we might reflect your love and kindness to
all with whom we meet or connect this day.

Lord of the day
We give you our time.

PART 2

Confronting Busyness

In the next five sessions we will look in different ways at "busyness". A time-wise approach says that it is important to understand it before we address it. Take a deep breath before you begin. This section is quite hard-hitting.

> *We all know what "busy" looks like: quick movements, short sentences, darting eye glances and, dare I say it, self-importance. But what does "not busy" look like?*

SESSION 4
Busyness—the Disease and the Medicine

The demands of church leadership today are often overwhelming. In the short term they lead to busyness and, if left unchecked, long-term busyness can lead to disappointment, disillusionment and even burn-out.

Busyness is not a solution to the problem of time pressure or time poverty. Busyness is another problem. It might be helpful to think of busyness as a disease, or even an epidemic. It seems to threaten just about everyone in ministry today. You can call that disease by different names, for instance, "hurry sickness".[5] I just call it "busy" or "busyness", but let's be clear, when you read the word "busy" here it does not mean "good", "important", "hard pressed", or "to be pitied", it means "sick".

No one likes being sick. It's not just that the symptoms are painful and distressing, there is also the guilt. You have to stop what you are doing and learn how to receive help from others. Busy people find this especially difficult. One of the reasons they are busy is that they like doing things, being in charge, taking responsibility and being productive. Control freaks and micro-managers are almost invariably very busy people. It goes with the territory. Some busy people even like it when others put more demands on them. They enjoy the limelight and the pressure to be productive. Their thinking goes like this: "If you want something done, ask a busy person. So hey, ask me. Please ask me!"

Not that busy people are necessarily productive. It is *effective* people who are productive, and effective does not mean busy. All effective people have busy spells, but it does not become for them a way of life. They do not need to be busy to feel good. They need to be busy because circumstances demand it for a while. However, effective people know that being busy, while it is inevitable in a crisis, has a huge downside. When we are busy we become reactive rather than responsive, we get stressed and stop listening, we pay attention to ourselves too much and to others too little.

Busy people also seem to transmit a number of messages—whether they know it or not. These messages are not the kind of messages which make for healthy, sustainable or developing ministry. For instance, busy people give the impression that they believe themselves to be important, or at least "more important than you", whoever "you" are. They also more or less consciously send the message, "No! This is *not* the right time."

It might not be the right time, of course. For example, it is not a good idea to ask a fireman who is trying to train his hose on a burning car for directions to the nearest sweet shop. Yet ministry does involve working with time and events in such a way that creates a *right time* for everything that really matters. We cannot do this while our attention is divided between the impressive flurry of our own hyperactivity and whatever it is that we are meant to be doing next. Or are late for. Or which we have forgotten about but which is nagging away in the back of our mind.

Time for Reflection

◆ Listen out for people using the word "busy" about themselves or about you. What do you hear when someone else says "I'm busy"?
◆ Take a little time to think about the word "busy". Write a few sentences which begin: "I am busy because . . ."

Food for Thought

I was also struck by the lack of busyness among all the clergy I met (in Romania) and the almost complete absence of diaries. There seemed to be more space to be human in. We are obviously ministering in different contexts, but for a church that is too often task driven, and imitates the commercial world in its drive to be productive, I felt such a lack of unnecessary activity was prophetic.[6]

Why Not . . . ?

Think of someone who you would really like to visit but know you are not going to . . . and give them a phone call. It will be good for them and it will be good for your conscience. Ten minutes on the phone could make all the difference.

SESSION 5
Ask the Horse

In her book *Time Management for Unmanageable People*, Ann McGee-Cooper says that we are suffering an epidemic of "hurry sickness". She quotes a communications specialist at an Electronic Data Systems company who says that her son has "a working vocabulary of seven words . . . two of them are 'hurry' and 'go'!"[7] As the quote implies, "hurry sickness" is infectious—parents willingly inflicting it on their young children, for instance.

When infected by hurry sickness we expect to do more and to do it faster, and so we shrink or eliminate our refreshment breaks. In particular we remove from our lives things like play and contemplation. We forget to take time to let go, engage our imaginations, see the funny side of things and have a laugh. The point is not new. The twentieth-century poet William Henry Davies wrote about it in his poem *Leisure*. The final lines speak volumes.

> A poor life this if, full of care,
> we have no time to stand and stare.

Not having time to stand and stare robs life of meaning and pleasure. It can also be counterproductive because it precipitates even more time anxiety and busyness.

Many see busyness as a fact of modern life, and there is no doubt that conditions of late or post-modernity do encourage this sense of things running out of control. More and more people find themselves living in the crowded fast lane of the motorway. But it is not an entirely new experience.

An ancient Zen story tells of someone standing bedside a path in the desert. He sees a great ball of sand rising into the air on the horizon. It is moving. It is coming towards him fast. He hears the sound of a horse's hooves. Sure enough, the horse appears. On the horse sits another man, holding on for dear life. The first man shouts to the rider, "Where are you going? What's the rush?" The man on the house shouts back, "I don't know, ask the horse".

In Session 3 I described busyness as a disease. You might have felt that to be a little harsh, but writing in his book *The Contemplative Pastor* Eugene Peterson is even more astringent.

> The word *busy* is the symptom not of commitment but of betrayal. It is not
> devotion but defection. The adjective *busy* set as a modifier to *pastor* should
> sound to our ears like *adulterous* to characterize a wife or *embezzling* to describe

a banker. It is an outrageous scandal, a blasphemous affront.[8]

These are strong words. They assert that it is an affront to the grace and providence of God that the only way in which we can achieve all that needs to be done is by adopting the combination of attitudes and behaviours that we call "busy". It is also a slur on our own capacity to discern appropriate priorities carefully. If busy is the disease, and Reverend Busy is the patient, time wisdom is the therapy—and it begins right now.

Time for Reflection

Suppose the word "busy" did not exist. Go through your sentences from Session 4 changing the word busy for "happy", "fulfilled", "important", "faithful" or "good".

When you have done this think about what you are trying to say by using the word "busy" about yourself or others. What do you mean when you say that you are busy?

Food for Thought

Jesus said to his disciples, "Therefore I tell you, do not worry about your life, what you will eat, or about your body, what you will wear. For life is more than food, and the body more than clothing. Consider the ravens: they neither sow nor reap, they have neither storehouse nor barn, and yet God feeds them. Of how much more value are you than the birds! And can any of you by worrying add a single hour to your span of life? If then you are not able to do so small a thing as that, why do you worry about the rest? Consider the lilies, how they grow: they neither toil nor spin; yet I tell you, even Solomon in all his glory was not clothed like one of these. But if God so clothes the grass of the field, which is alive today and tomorrow is thrown into the oven, how much more will he clothe you—you of little faith![9]

Why Not . . . ?

Work out which of all the things you have to do this week is the least attractive . . . and just do it for the joy of not having it on your mind any more.

SESSION 6

Busy or Stressed?

Reflecting on the last two sessions I wonder whether they are a little bit harsh. I have two reasons for this. Sometimes the word "busy" is not one that we choose but which we have thrust upon us. It is as if people want us to be busy—for reasons of their own. The issue here is whether we capitulate or resist. My suggestion is that a time-wise approach requires us to resist because "busy" is such an unhelpful word. It is a word which lacks insight and which suggests a lack of control. Think about it. If someone said to you "how are you—I expect you have lost the plot at this time of year" you might not be quite as pleased as if they suggest you are busy. Yet maybe that is what they mean!

The second reason I feel that it may have been a little harsh is because not long after writing it I experienced a period of time in which I was indeed busy. I had little choice but to try to get more done than it was reasonable to expect in a limited time. During these few weeks I found it hard to resist the suggestion of others that I was "busy" despite everything that I have said—and which I believe to be true.

My reflections on this are as follows:

This episode had a number of unconnected causes. It was just that a variety of things cropped up and needed to be resolved by me at the same time as I had already scheduled a reasonable amount of work.

What I actually experienced during this time—and the reason I used the b-word, was not busyness exactly but stress. I was worried about the consequences of not achieving some of the tasks or of letting people down. For one reason or another, things got to me a bit.

The good news from this story is that after a few weeks the episode came to an end. During it I did find enough time and wisdom to take a step back and reschedule a few things and that took some pressure off. The important things were done to a reasonable standard and, while I was at it, I set up a few systems that would help prevent such a collision of expectations from happening again.

It was essentially a bit of a work crisis. The way I coped was to name it as such to myself and to do all that I could to get to the far side of it in one piece.

The problem for many in ministry today is, I think, that they have maintained an approach to ministry which is highly responsive (if not reactive) in a situation of significantly increased potential demand—often serving in a string of parishes across a number of communities and maybe being responsible for several church buildings. This means that the likelihood of a time of crisis which is stressful, and in which busy behaviour is the only way of coping, is more and more common.

This reality, this vulnerability, needs to be analysed and understood so that the minister can live in a way that is sustainable and so that they can offer a form of ministry that is effective.

Flourishing ministers will always have times of crisis, periods of stress and busy patches, whether they are days, weeks or even longer. The difference is that those who develop some time wisdom will be working to reduce these periods and to establish a norm which is liveable.

Flourishing ministers will also see these periods of crisis as valuable opportunities to get a lot done and maybe turn some significant corners. In a crisis the heat is turned up and decisions that seemed just too difficult are at last made. In my recent crisis period I tidied both my study at home and my diocesan office. These are tasks I find very difficult, but in the heat of it all I was able to make the "file or discard" decision much more easily. Having two tidy rooms after an hour's work made coping with the crisis much less stressful. It was symbolic of my getting a grip.

The other advantage of such displacement activities (provided that they are actually productive) is that they can give the back of your mind some thinking time so that you might address the real issues more wisely. They also give you something to do with that extra bit of adrenaline which makes you want to get on with it—when you are still not yet sure what *it* is. It may be that one of the issues you are handling requires not decisiveness, but patience and care—it is often like that in ministry. In which case rather than kick the cat you might as well tidy the study when you get home.

Time for Reflection

Think back to a time when you were experiencing a crisis of too much to do and not enough time to do it in. You might find it helpful to scroll back though your diary. Suppose you had to describe how it began and what brought that episode to an end. What would you say?

Food for Thought

"Never waste a good crisis!" The phrase has been used by many politicians. A less well known but equally wise phrase is "never waste good anger".

Sometimes events beyond our control, or our reactions to them, make something possible that had always seemed improbable. Maybe this is what the word "moment" means and why, as some have claimed, true leadership happens "in the moment".

Why Not . . . ?

Put an absolute time limit on the next meeting you are chairing.

SESSION 7
White Rabbit Behaviour

If we are ever to get beyond busyness we are going to have to be clever and cunning, optimistic and opportunistic. It will involve a number of strategies and tactics, but the first is very simple and can be worked on at a number of levels and in a number of ways. It is the method of not looking busy.

We all know what "busy" looks like: quick movements, short sentences, darting glances and, dare I say it, self-importance. There is not much listening and no peripheral vision. Busy people rush off looking at their watches like the White Rabbit in *Alice in Wonderland* and muttering, "I'm late, I'm late".

But what does "not busy" look like? This is a major challenge for those in ministry today. The reality will probably be that you have more on your mind than you are ever going to achieve and yet as soon as you begin to let that be shown to others, you move yourself away from the relationship of openness and availability which is integral to ministry.

The list below gives fourteen suggestions which might help you give the impression of *not* being busy. Try them out, but not all at once! Keep coming back to the list and see if you can try a new one.

There is some psychology behind my suggestion. We know that human minds are very significantly influenced by their bodies. If you hold a pencil cross ways between your teeth (so that you smile) you will find a story funnier than if you hold the same pencil lengthwise so that you purse your lips. So, if you engage in White Rabbit behaviour you will soon start to believe that it is appropriate and that you are both busier and far more important than you are. The reverse is also true: if you consciously adopt some un-busy behaviour you will begin to find the busyness falling away.

14 ways to give the impression of not being too busy

1. Don't rush about.
2. Walk positively and purposefully.
3. Never say "I am very busy".
4. Never say "yes" when people ask if you are busy.
5. Refute anyone who says, "I thought you would be too busy to . . ."
6. Ignore anything marked "URGENT".
7. Always be on time—even if it is *just* on time.
8. Never sigh on arrival or say "phew".

9.   Keep saying to yourself, "no one is indispensable—not even me".
10. Never tell people what you are about to do next or "rush on to".
11. Don't play diaryopoly[10] with your colleagues.
12. Never say, "I have three meetings to attend all at the same time".
13. Don't tell people that you have missed your day off.
14. Do tell people what you do when you have some free time.

There is another way to use this list, but it requires a little more courage from you—and the time of someone you trust. Give your trusted person the list and ask them to tell you truthfully the extent to which you display White Rabbit behaviour. We are often unaware of our worst habits. After an initial conversation around the list you might want to schedule another appointment in a month's time to have another look. If you are cured then, that's fine. Otherwise, you will need to keep working at it. Be assured: the pressure is on to make you feel stressed and look busy. Resist it.

Time for Reflection

•   What do you think when you see White Rabbit behaviour in others? What do you *feel* about it?
•   Which White Rabbit behaviours are you most prone to yourself?

Food for Thought

Arriving at the crematorium to take my first funeral, I found that the cortege was already there. The back door of the hearse was open and the coffin half way through, ready to be lifted. The mourners were standing around, waiting.

I had been driven there by my training incumbent and was very anxious. Not wanting to delay things any further I moved quickly to get out of the car as it was being parked. "Don't rush", came the calm but firm voice of the vicar. "You're not late. They're early." So I steadied myself and carried on confidently, at a calming pace. A good lesson.

Why Not . . . ?

Write your own caricature of a minister who is having a White Rabbit day. This is how it begins: "Reverend Rush was in a hurry. S/he had *so* much to do and so little time in which to do it all . . ."

SESSION 8
Where Does it All Go?

"I don't know where all the time went, the day has just flown by." It might have been me speaking, or it might have been you. It might have been a good day or it might have been a bad one. If this is what you can say every night then the chances are that you are not being as time-wise as you need to be.

Most time management experts suggest that it is helpful to keep some kind of log of your time as you try to begin to get a grip on its management. However, many suggestions of keeping a time log are over-ambitious and will put you off before you have started. Alex Mackenzie, who wrote *The Time Trap*, suggests that it should be a log of "every time you shift your attention". Frankly I don't understand how anyone could do that level of analysis without bringing their whole life to a halt. So I am not suggesting that you try.

However, I am suggesting that you do some kind of analysis or audit of where the time goes. I have not done this very often, but I do it every now and again and on one occasion in parish ministry it was a very important exercise in pulling me back from the brink. It was a time when my responsibilities had become more and more demanding and I had taken on a number of extra tasks. I was running fast just to stand still and no matter what I did, it seemed that there was more than I could manage.

Happily, I had a wise thought one day. It was, like all wise thoughts, very simple. "I can't go on like this." You may have had the same thought yourself. You may even be having it now.

I can't remember the precise details of how I got out of my predicament or how long it took, but I can remember the core ingredients.

First, I drew a table on a piece of A4 paper (see Figure 2). It had seven columns and three rows: a column for each day of the week and a row for morning, afternoon and evening.

Second, I came up with a rough classification of the various activities I engaged in. There were nine ranging from "Worship", "Office/Admin", "Church Meetings", "Community" to "Diocese". I had two kinds of preparation on my list: "spiritual preparation" and what I called "caretaking".

Third, I jotted into each session of the table the category of activity that took up most of the time (Figure 3).

Fourth, I persuaded a colleague in a nearby parish to do the same activity and to meet with me once a month to talk it through.

	SUNDAY	MONDAY	TUESDAY	WEDNESDAY	THURSDAY	FRIDAY	SATURDAY
MORNING							
AFTERNOON							
EVENING							

Figure 2: Blank weekly plan table

	SUNDAY	MONDAY	TUESDAY	WEDNESDAY	THURSDAY	FRIDAY	SATURDAY
MORNING	Worship	Office/Admin	Day off	Office/Admin	Community	Office/Admin	Caretaking
AFTERNOON	Pastoral	Community	Day off	Diocese	Spiritual preparation	Pastoral	Social
EVENING	Worship	Church Meeting	Day off	Church Meeting	Pastoral	Choir, then family	Family

Figure 3: A Week in the Parish

That's the story in a nutshell, but a few more details are relevant.

When I first drew up one of these weekly tables and tried to fill it in, I found it extremely difficult. I was not sure what categories would work and had to go though several attempts before I could find categories that made sense of my ministerial use of time.

So the first few tables in my log were very messy with lots of entries in each of the sections of the tables. As time went by a kind of calmness and order began to descend on the table. I tended to focus a session on a type of activity and to devote myself to that for a while. I also found it easier to cross out whole sections and to work fewer of them. It settled down to 13–16 per week.

Every week I also did a quick tot-up of the number of sessions spent on each activity. A typical week had about 2.5 sessions of "worship", two of these on a Sunday, and 8.5 sessions were of "office/admin". There were also one or two "pastoral" sessions. 1.5 of "local community", one of "diocesan commitment", one of "caretaking-type preparation", one of "spiritual preparation", and one of "social", that is, time with church members or parishioners with no particular aim in mind or pastoral need being addressed.

What this does not reveal is how much time I spent over meals, in prayer or study, but you can guess the story. With the monitoring and analysis, even at this level, so came a greater calm across the whole of life.

Perhaps the most surprising thing about this analysis was the amount of "office/admin" time, or, to be more accurate, the number of sessions that I labelled in this way. There are several reasons for this. One of which is that there was a lot of that sort of work to do in that parish at that time and for various reasons I needed to be doing it. Second is that the admin base of the parish was an office in a community centre next to the church, and by being there I was doing far more than rotas. In fact, I didn't do rotas. Nor did I really do very much basic admin at all. So in my particular case, office/admin had a degree of outreach, community engagement and pastoral work built into it. That matters. If I had spent all of those sessions locked away in the vicarage my ministry would have been very different. The desk work would have been done more effectively, perhaps, but the interruptions would have been far less productive. In reading my own time analysis I had to realise that office/admin actually meant "helping to staff the parish pastoral drop-in centre".

To summarise: this session has not been about planning your time, but *about the benefits of monitoring where your time goes.* My experience is that you do not need to do this in a very detailed way to begin to get significant benefits. A rough and ready analysis will teach you a lot and encourage you to bring order and shape to your day and week; yet that is not the end of it. Such a process can also bring order to the monthly and annual cycles in which we are necessarily involved—and which can easily begin to confuse us if we do not keep a careful eye on them.

Time for Reflection

- If you were asked to say where your time went would you be able to identify up to five main areas of activity?
- What do you hope the balance of time between the various areas might be?
- What would someone who knows you well say?

Food for Thought

It took centuries of dialogue between God and his people Israel before their language was fit to bear that Word of perfect love, just as it took centuries before the English language was ready for Shakespeare to write Hamlet. It takes just nine months for a child to be ready to come from the womb, but it took innumerable generations of prophets and scribes, mothers and fathers, poets and lawgivers, before the language of God's people was ready for the Word of love to be made flesh.[11]

Why Not . . . ?

Find someone who will share with you a time-monitoring exercise for a month. (Is it because you are a tiny bit afraid that they might do more hours than you?)

Time for Everything

For everything there is a season, and a time
for every matter under heaven:
> *a time to be born, and a time to die;*
> *a time to plant, and a time to pluck up what is planted;*
> *a time to kill, and a time to heal;*
> *a time to break down, and a time to build up;*
> *a time to weep, and a time to laugh;*
> *a time to mourn, and a time to dance;*
> *a time to throw away stones, and a*
> > *time to gather stones together;*
> *a time to embrace, and a time to refrain from embracing;*
> *a time to seek, and a time to lose;*
> *a time to keep, and a time to throw away;*
> *a time to tear, and a time to sew;*
> *a time to keep silence, and a time to speak;*
> *a time to love, and a time to hate;*
> *a time for war, and a time for peace.*

ECCLESIASTES 3.1–8

Three Parables

We are never too old to enjoy a story! The point of parables is that they stick in the mind and so influence our attitudes and behaviours. There are some important principles wrapped up here.

> *An admiral talking about leadership once said that the two most important words are, "you decide".*

SESSION 9

The Parable of the Bucket

A father was on a beach playing with his children. Tired of making sandcastles he decided to set them a challenge. "Let's see how much we can get into the bucket", he said.

Child number one went off and filled the bucket with sand. "I have got most in the bucket", she said. "It's got millions of grains of sand."

Child number two said, "I've got most in the bucket: it's got lots of stones and each one is loads bigger than a grain of sand".

Child number three was still busy. She had found a large rock and put it in the middle of the bucket, then she added some smaller ones that filled in around it. Then she filled it up with sand and gravel before decorating the top with shells.

The dad beamed with delight at the children and declared them all winners because each of their buckets were full to the brim.

That dad was a good and kind parent but a more objective observer might have seen it differently. Especially if they had realised that this was a parable of time wisdom.

This is what it means.

The bucket is a day and as each child fills the bucket differently, so each person fills their day differently.

The bucket filled to the brim with sand is a day filled with a million tiny tasks. This is the "one thing after the other" scenario. The day is full, the person is busy and exhausted. Looking back over the day they can see that there was never any time for the big things because the little ones took up every waking hour.

Child number two's bucket contains a number of stones, but nothing else. This is the person who puts a few things in their diary and goes from one to another, doing them dutifully. They fail to notice that there are lots of little things that might be done in the gaps between them. In terms of the parish priest, this is the person who does the school assembly, the home communions, and the meetings, but neglects the phone call, the sending of the card, and the 5-minute visit.

Child number three begins with a big stone and then packs around it medium sized, different shaped and finally, tiny things before at the end adding a flourish of decoration. This is the person who takes a strategic approach to life but at the same time knows that the little things matter. So the big stone is perhaps the parish's main project for the year or even the decade: the new church plant, the building or restoration project, the amalgamation with a neighbouring parish, or the creation of a new parish strategy or vision. After this the medium sized tasks get packed in—all different shapes and sizes—before the tiny, last minute, responsive grains of sand-like activities all get packed in around, in any space available. Surprisingly there is quite a lot of it. Last, but not least, the whole bucket is beautified by a few shells. This child knows that appearance matters and is not too busy to take another few moments.

Child number three, I need hardly underline, represents the time-wise adult. Time wisdom tells us that if we start out with all the tiny tasks the bucket will soon be full of them and this will mean that there is no room for the big stone in the middle. Yet time wisdom also tells us that if we just put in the medium-sized stones then equally there will be no space for the one big stone. It also tells us that if we concentrate only on the medium-sized stones then much will be lost at the grains of sand level.

This parable is a variant of the "cookie jar experiment" which time management trainers often perform at their sessions. How do you get all this stuff into a jar? The answer is "in order of size". If you put the little stuff in first the big stuff will never fit, and so it is with both your diary and your life.

The point is well made and needs to be taken on board. On the other hand, time wisdom will also tell us that often to put a great big lump in the middle of the diary is impossible, and that if we do set aside a very large amount of time it often gets lost. This can happen because, when it comes to it, we are so much in the habit of doing small responsive things that we find some more to do (I can think of many a day off spoilt like that) or that we are just too locked into doing medium sized things that we can't take on the big one—it is too frightening, too onerous.

Finally, notice that child number three took longer to fill the bucket than the other two. That's true too. We need to factor in the time to fill the bucket, to manage the diary so that it reflects our priorities and values and allows us to make a great difference in little ways on a daily basis, in medium-sized ways on a weekly and monthly basis and in a big way over a period of several months or years. Ministry involves living simultaneously on several time scales. It is wise and prudent if we recognise this and try to organise our lives to minister on each scale, if not every day, then every week.

Time for Reflection

- What is your biggest stone?
- What is your sand?

Food for Thought

Time is emotion. For instance, have you ever noticed how disproportionately delighted people are if something ends a few minutes early? And the same people can be equally disproportionate in their irritation if it goes on a few minutes longer than anticipated.

Time-wise leaders often say, "And so we are going to end a few minutes early." How do they manage that?

Why Not . . . ?

Write down three things you would do if you had three hours to do as you wish this week.

SESSION 10
Elephant Eating for Beginners

Let's go back to the beach for a minute. There is another child with a bucket. He has his eye on a lovely stone. It is beautiful smooth pebble with an intricate pattern of graining and dazzling colouration. The child rushes to the water's edge and gets some water to throw over it. He admires it and wants to get it into his bucket. He can just about pick it up but, sadly, the stone is bigger than the bucket. This young man really wants to move the stone, but it is just too big. There is nothing he can do about it.

Sometimes that's the way it is. The project, the work, the ministry is immensely attractive and important. We can see its potential and we can present it in such a way that it looks wonderful to others, but some things are just too big for us. It is wise to know when the stone is bigger than the bucket. We can waste a lot of time either trying to force it in where it does not fit, getting frustrated about it, or calling meetings in the hope that somehow or other someone else might be able to expand the bucket. Plastic buckets do have a little "give", but not much. If you try to force something too big into a bucket you end up splitting it, and a split bucket is useless.

However, charming as they can be, every metaphor has its limits and when we reach them we need to think of a new metaphor. Some tasks are not like stones, but like elephants. That is, they are very big and perhaps frightening. They are also very daunting indeed if the task is (with apologies to vegetarians) to eat the elephant.

So this is the question—and it is an important one in time management courses—"How do you eat an elephant?" The answer? One bite at a time.

I once watched a TV documentary in which an elephant was eaten in the wild. A camera crew set up near a dead elephant and observed. Needless to say the elephant was indeed eaten, but here's the fascinating bit: most of it was not consumed by the hyenas or the big cats that came along to gorge on free flesh, but by a mighty army of maggots. Absolutely millions of them. It was a creepy but magnificent spectacle and it illustrates the lesson. If you want to dispose of an elephant corpse in an efficient and ecologically creative way don't send for the hyenas, send for the flies!

The tasks we face, however, cannot be dealt with by natural processes that happen whether we like it or not. That is precisely why human beings have intelligence and communities have leaders. If you want to achieve a big task then you have to bring some real time wisdom to the planning of it. Here are two critical principles:

- You will only get a big project done if you plan it into your time schedule before you put in the medium and little things.
- If a project is sufficiently large then it will need to be broken up into smaller chunks before you can even get it into the empty bucket.

While working on this book I was involved in the planning of a multi-million-pound development project. In one area of the work there was very little progress for six weeks. Part of the solution was to move away from monthly meetings with a lot of people present to consult about the project to weekly meetings attended by a smaller number of people. Sure enough, the project began to make better progress. Time wisdom often tells you this: use the "take a little and often" method, take small manageable steps, and approach your deadlines cautiously and from afar.

Time wisdom is also the wisdom of the wild, the wisdom of nature, of ecology. The real answer to the question of how elephants get eaten is not "one mouthful at a time". Elephants get eaten most effectively by a complex and leaderless team of tiny, tiny creatures. It is not a very attractive metaphor perhaps—but then again neither is tearing into the flesh of an elephant like a hungry hyena. Apparently impossible tasks require of us not only the careful management of our time. They will only ever get done if we engage our imaginations and find a way of making what seemed like a personal project a team effort.

Time for Reflection

- What's the biggest single task you have ever had to face?
- Spend a while thinking through how you worked at it over a period of time. Might any of the work have been shared with others? Did it overwhelm you? In the end, did most of it get done by an army of maggots?

Food for Thought

When I was learning how to sight-read, my music teacher used to say, "Don't worry about the notes, concentrate on the timing."

It's scary how many areas of life there are where this is true. It is a negative thing, of course. Get the timing wrong and even the most carefully thought-through plan can crumble to nothing.

Why Not . . . ?

Spend an hour reading through last year's diary and get a sense of where the time all went. Maybe you could make two short lists: "Glad that I invested time on . . ." and "Not sure that time was well spent on . . ."

SESSION 11
Taking the Monkey

One of the most vivid time wisdom lessons I was ever given happened one afternoon over the phone. I was talking to another parish priest about something which I cannot recall and for some reason that I cannot recollect when he told me about what he called "monkey business". It was, he assured me, the curse of effective ministry. I asked him to explain.

"There you are," he says, "walking through the street or maybe through the churchyard, and you stop and chat with someone. During the conversation they tell you what they are concerned about. You listen, share the concern and walk away, somehow with responsibility for doing something about this concern. Recognise the story?".

I recognised the story very well. It seemed to be the story of ministerial life. You wander around, meeting people while they get unburdened, and while you get loaded up.

"It's monkey business", he said. "People often have these monkeys on their shoulders just waiting to jump onto someone else. And monkeys are quite gregarious. They like to be with lots of other monkeys and so, if they see you already have a few, they jump across all the more quickly."

It was a revelation to me. It described exactly what was happening, time and time again. I was young and kind and nice then and I am sure I spent a lot of time and effort not only accepting monkeys onto my shoulders but actually enticing them across. I quite liked the lively little creatures. The trouble, however, is that the monkeys need feeding, they take time and attention and if they don't get it they start to quarrel and fight. Before long they are dominating your life and you can't think about anything else.

This monkey metaphor first saw the light of day in an article in the *Harvard Business Review* in 1974 by William Oncken Jr and Donald L. Wass. It is one of HBR's two bestselling reprints and its author made a name and something of a brand for himself through it. Steven Covey has said that he more than once saw him walking through an airport lounge with a stuffed monkey on his shoulder. The article is about the way in which subordinates in an organization tend to pile their superiors with difficulties which then burden the senior person while the subordinate has less to worry about. Of course it is not quite like that in the parish, but it is remarkable the way in which the Church seems to require those who are given leadership positions to accept monkeys.

As for me, I only needed to hear the story once to begin to get the message. I will not say that I never catch a monkey, but awareness that there are monkeys ready to jump is never far from my mind.

I once heard an Admiral talking about leadership. In his view the two most important words for a leader to use are, "you decide".

It is phrase that stops those monkeys in their tracks. It is not always possible or fair to say it, but maybe it is a phrase we could use more often.

The key to managing the monkey business in ministry is to retain some control of the monkey-jumping. It is absolutely *not* a requirement of ministry that you have to leave a conversation saying "I will get back to you", or, "I will think about that", or "I will . . . anything". It is much more realistic to say, "do get back to me about this if you need to". Or even, "Let me know how *x* is when you have been to see them."

Time for Reflection

◆ Think back over the last 48 hours and see how many monkeys jumped onto your shoulders. (A monkey is a responsibility to do something which you have acquired from someone else whom, had they not encountered you, would have still had it on their back.)

◆ How many monkeys do you want? How many can you carry at any one time?

◆ Is it impossible that you are just a little bit *too* nice, kind and well-meaning and that as a result you are carrying round a whole zoo of monkeys on your shoulders?

Food for Thought

This is an exchange between an American reporter and Michael Ramsey, Archbishop of Canterbury.[12]

Q. Have you said your prayers this morning?
R. Yes.
Q. What did you say in your prayers?
R. I talked to God.
Q. How long did you talk to God?
R. I talked to God for one minute. But it took me twenty-nine minutes to get there.

Why Not . . . ?

De-clutter the top of your desk—and make sure all the drawers can close too.

What is Time?

When St Augustine asked himself this question, he answered that, "Provided no one asks me, I know." But he went on to confess that, "If I want to explain to an enquirer, I do not know."[13] Many will identify with this paradox. We are both at one with time, and yet mystified and perplexed by it.

One way to think of time is to imagine that it has a multi-layered texture; that there is a geology of time. At the deeper levels we have the primitive and natural—the raw—aspects of time. Nearer the surface are those aspects of time that are the product of human activity and ingenuity.

At the deepest level there is cosmic time; time as determined by the nature of the cosmos in general and the solar system in particular: the calendar of years and seasons, day and night. Cosmic time has been noted, interpreted and labelled in different ways down the years and so we live with a multiplicity of calendars, both religious and secular. Sometimes these calendars are in tension, sometimes they are synchronous.

The invention of the clock created another layer of time. It is hard for us now to imagine a clock-less day. As Zimbardo and Boyd have commented, "We have created and so completely adapted to clock time that many of us feel naked without a wrist watch."[14]

Today there is perhaps another layer of time. It might be called "instant time". It is faster and more demanding than clock time and has as its goal the elimination of gaps of time. 24-hour news and Twitter are more recent manifestations of this. In "instant time" there is no delay between event and knowledge of the event. It has great advantages, but also real dangers. The main one, perhaps, is that it encourages a culture of reactivity. It pushes us to rely on reflexes rather than our capacity to reflect.

Time wisdom involves understanding the importance and power of each of these main layers in the geology of time. It recognises the need to respect the demands of each level while not seeing any level as the only one. All levels matter, and so do the interactions between the levels and the temporal phenomena caused by the impact that any level has on the others.

This geological model applies to *chronos*. But it also suggests something about *kairos*. Kairos—the moment of opportunity, the right time, is perhaps a product of the way in which these layers interact to create opportune occasions. There are many other temporal factors that might go to make up a *kairos*: your age, for instance, or your health or the clock or calendar time that has elapsed since another significant event.

What makes a *kairos* is too subtle and complex to predict. It is far more difficult to tell what time is coming than what the weather will be. Time wise people know this, and yet are vigilant to the possibility that an unexpected *kairos* might appear, like an earthquake, at any time. They also realise that there is nothing they can do to hasten or delay it.

Four Techniques

These four methods can quickly become skills if you understand how they work and put in a bit of effort as you make up your diary and plan longer-term projects. None of these are rocket science and you might well be using them already, whether in a thought-out way or intuitively.

Time wisdom is all about being appropriately proactive and appropriately responsive.

SESSION 12
Listing

Towards the beginning of his wonderful book *God's Companions*, Samuel Wells says something about its form: "The principle rhetorical device used in this book is the list. I simply intend to overwhelm the reader with examples".[15] The device, I suggest, was well chosen. Lists have a tremendous capacity to overwhelm, and therein lies both the power and the weaknesses of many time management courses.

The basic idea of many time management courses is for you to make a list of all the things you need to do. You then prioritise them. Then you work through the list methodically, ticking things off in order as you achieve them. The concept is that if you follow this method you will, sooner or later, accomplish all of your tasks.

I have to admit that this is something that I do. In fact I don't think I would be able to get through the demands of my week without it. List writing is fundamental to time wisdom, but there is more to writing lists than meets the eye. For one thing, while some people find that writing a list helps them cope with overwhelming demands, others find that the list itself can be overwhelming—as Wells exploits in his book.

Ask some people to write a list of things they need to do, or should do, and half an hour later you will come back and find them still at it. They will have used up one piece of paper and gone on the hunt for more—finding scrap and old envelopes from around their not very tidy workspace. Although they hate the challenge once they get started there is no stopping them. They have been challenged to be creative and creative is what they will be. "Oh! And I really should . . ." and another thing goes on the list.

I describe this as if it were funny but funny is only part of the story. There is a deep problem here in that such a list is both exciting *and* overwhelming. The poor list-writer uses up all their energy in creating it. Once in existence it does not empower so much as oppress them. A "to do" list with 34 items on it, many of them representing things laden either with positive emotion (I'd love to do that) or negative emotion (I feel so guilty that I have not done it already) is a terrible burden. Standard time management advice would be to begin to organise the list into priorities.[16] You might as well ask someone to edit their own writing. Every word (every item on the list) is absolutely vital. Prioritising is an advanced skill.

Now I want you to step back a bit from what you have just read. I suggest that some readers will have read those paragraphs with horror. Others will have read them with recognition. For some people the list is a calming tool, for others the list is a powerful presence which can be friend or foe and can flip from one to the other quite quickly.

There is an important lesson to be learned, whether or not you like the idea of the to-do list. It is that there is no one who has written or trained people about time management who will say that it is a bad idea to write down the things that you need to do. That is because it is a very good idea. The trouble is that although the idea is good, the practice can be difficult, or even frightening.

So here is an idea to make the prospect of list writing more palatable to *listophobes*. Rather than try the one-column to-do list, why not try the two-column to-do list?[17] The way this works is quite simple and involves you in nothing more complicated than drawing a line vertically down the middle of the page. The left hand column you can call "essential", "vital", or whatever you like. The right hand column is "less vital" or "not quite so essential". I use this method, calling the left hand column "MUST" and the right hand column "MAY" (Figure 4).

Curiously, although apparently more complicated, the two-column to-do list is a lot less stressful to prepare than the one-column list. It's worth a go, anyway.

MONDAY 16TH APRIL 2012	
MUST	MAY

Figure 4: Two-column "To Do" list

The two-column to-do list also has another advantage: the possibility of the horizontal slide.

With traditional to-do lists an item is either on or off; it is either waiting to be done or not yet done. With the two-column list it is possible for items to be bumped from the MAY column to the MUST column, or perhaps the other way. This is another way in which the two-column list is more realistic; and therefore much more appropriate for those in ministry where the idea that you can live a life free of interruptions is sheer fantasy. Many of the things we need to do come at us from left field and knock our plans about. The two-column list is drawn up with this expectation in mind.

Time for Reflection

- How do you feel about lists? Do you find preparing them calming or stressful?
- What would you do if one morning you realised that you have more to do than is actually possible?
- Can you think of a colleague who might have a very different response to lists and list making than you? Why not arrange to have a chat with them about the way they cope with an overwhelming number of demands.

Food for Thought

In the Bible the *kairos* exists in tension with the view of time as *chronos*. *Chronos* is clock time, the succession of events from past to future. Although the gospel writers use this term as part of their narration, we never hear it used by Jesus. When Jesus talks about time he emphatically uses the word *kairos*. *Kairos* is the very opposite of chronos, not time in general, but particular moments of time—the "hours", "days", "seasons" of history. The point here us not the direction of time or its chronological end (*telos*). *Kairos* is the epiphany of time, time distilled into moments or intersections. *Kairos* is a transcendence of *chronos*: *chronos* shows us the series, while *kairos* shows us the episodes.[18]

Why Not . . . ?

Write a short list of things that people expect you to do but actually you cannot. It's your, "Sorry, I can't do that" list.

SESSION 13

Clumping

In Session 8 we looked at the way in which monitoring our use of time can have the effect of helping us create more coherent and effective work sessions by clumping together similar tasks. Time wisdom involves extensive use of the technique of clumping, but clumping is not the only way to schedule important parts of our ministry or tasks to be done. There is lot to be said for "clearing" and "threading" in ministry too. We will look at clearing in Session 14 and threading in Session 15. In this session our focus is on clumping.

The psychology of clumping is very powerful. Relatively recent research shows that the amount of effort involved in moving from one demanding intellectual task to another is much more considerable than people used to think. Suppose you were busy sorting out some accounts for a Church charity. After ten minutes you put them to one side and begin work on a talk you are giving later that day. Then you begin to wonder about the meal you need to eat before going out to give the talk, which, as it happens, needs some preparation—so why not think about that a bit right now? Each of these tasks demands a certain amount of effort and energy, but do you notice that you have given yourself four extra tasks in that little work session? Each time you shift task you have to do the extra work of switching from one task to another. This is a great, but largely hidden, way of being *in*effective—of wasting time. I should know—I am an inveterate flitter.

Clumping is the opposite of channel-hopping on the TV. It is the attempt to draw together tasks, projects and bits of work so that the number of times you need to change channels is reduced. Channel hopping only happens when TVs have many channels and, crucially, a remote control. No one did it when it involved getting up and walking across the room and fiddling around with a dial. Your brain is more like an old-fashioned TV than a flat screen with a remote. It needs time to tune in, and probably more as you get older, and definitely more when the tasks you are dealing with are difficult, emotional or otherwise stressful. Which, I know, is just when you would so welcome a distraction that you would make one for yourself. Daniel Kahneman talks about getting up to make coffee or checking emails repeatedly when trying to write the difficult part of a book.[19] Of course this is sometimes a good thing. The walk to the kettle can be the moment in which the next thought comes or a muddle is resolved; or we might have actually become exhausted and need a break. But you know that that's not what we are talking about here. We are talking about what used to be called "lack of concentration".

Anyway, clumping is a technique designed to reduce the amount of switching between tasks that you need to do by putting similar tasks together. Clumping is essentially a way of organising your diary so that you group or connect similar things together and are not always lurching from one thing to another.

We have seen that the way our brains work means that clumping is a good idea when at the desk, whether it is in the office or the study. That is the psychology of it, but the physicality of clumping is good too. This point is very obvious but needs to be mentioned as it is a fundamental building block of any adequate time wisdom. Unless you are as bad at shopping as I am you do it whenever you visit the supermarket or town centre. That is, you go about things in such a way as to reduce to a minimum your travelling time between shelves or shops. The more you shop, the better you get at this, and the more annoyed you are when things are moved. The only point to be made here is to suggest that it is wise to try to take geography into account when you do your visiting. You are in a certain vicinity—make the most of it. What else can you do while you are there? It might not be on your "must do" list, but it could be on your "may do" list and make a real difference.

The old idea of a parish surgery is a simple form of clumping which works at both at the physical and the psychological levels. It may not be the best way to express openness and friendliness; it carries the message "you fit in with me", and in my parish situation I preferred to have a drop-in atmosphere at the parish office.

Clumping similar tasks in your diary and reducing the strain of mental task changing and the time involved in travelling here and there are positive ways to ensure that your time is being well spent in ministry.

Clumping takes a little time at the planning and preparation stage, but it is time well invested. It involves being proactive—but, as is becoming clear, time wisdom is all about being appropriately proactive and realistically responsive.

Time for Reflection

- Are you a channel-hopper when you watch TV? Are you a "flitter" when it comes to getting things done?
- Think about the electronic devices you use. Do they help you "clump" or do they demand that you change your focus of attention many times per hour?
- What scope might you have for clumping tasks next week?

Food for Thought

LORD, let me know my end,
>   and what is the measure of my days;
>   let me know how fleeting my life is.
You have made my days a few handbreadths,
>   and my lifetime is as nothing in your sight.
Surely everyone stands as a mere breath.
Surely everyone goes about like a shadow.
Surely for nothing they are in turmoil;
>   they heap up, and do not know who will gather.[20]

Why Not . . . ?

Think of someone who always seems to get their day off and to take plenty of holidays, and ask them how it's done.

SESSION 14
Clearing

Clearing is all about setting aside enough time to get into a piece of work and make a real impression. Some time management guides stress clearing above all else. Their point is easy to see: unless you make time for extended and deep thought, it probably won't happen. If you are in some sort of leadership role in a challenging situation which is often changing then to try to do it without significant thought is foolish.

Traditional time management books have a lot of positive ideas about organizing your life into chunks of usable time. However, looked at from the perspective of a responsive and engaged Christian minister, they don't always seem very plausible. These gurus just don't reckon on people dying or becoming ill, or the homeless turning up at the vicarage door.

Even if some of what they suggest sounds idealistic and naive the reason that they are suggesting it is sound. Extended periods of time for deeper and more thoughtful work which will impact over the longer term will not happen unless you make them happen.

Yet we need to take care as we do so. In my experience people in ministry can often oscillate quite wildly in this area. Sometimes they make little or no effort at all to clear even short amounts of time for extended thought or deeper work, but on other occasions they will insist that without a really extended time free from other pressures some particular plan will never be achieved. This sometimes lies behind the idea that if only a sabbatical were to be granted a great book would be written. "If only I had a really long stretch of time," they say, "I could read all these books and maybe write one." In reply I have sometimes asked, "But why don't you read little and often?" The response can be interesting. Sometimes it is a look which says, "Don't be stupid." Others are more honest and say, "I try, but I just fall asleep."

Extremely long periods of time are rarely as productive as we expect them to be. Our powers of concentration and our work disciplines are rarely as good in reality as they are in our fantasy. This is why most New Year's resolutions are in tatters before the wise men appear for Epiphany.

The answer to this is that we need to use our self-knowledge as we try to plan our work. While it is true that if we shift from task to task without clumping we end up getting much less done than we should—see Session 13—it is also true that we should be realistic about how long we should spend on one particular task. We also need to recognize that many of the more demanding things we do are going to take several sittings. That is why in the next session we will talk about threading. But we have not finished with clearing yet.

Clearing involves creating extended periods of time where it will be possible to give serious concentration to something that matters in the long term or which requires deep thought. This is necessary in any leadership role in a complex environment, but it is also important in terms of the spirituality of ministry. Jesus withdrew to pray. His radical ministry of availability and his profound, but not very wordy, teaching ministry were grounded in time away from others. "He withdrew to pray." We are not told how he prayed, but we might assume that it involved deeper reflective, extended, self-critical and God-aware thought. If Jesus did that, then why not you?

How do you then make sure that the space cleared in the diary remains cleared? That's a very real question. You can't put barbed wire or an electric fence around time. I have come across several different techniques that might be useful. Calling the cleared time "sermon preparation" might work for you as, even if you are not actually writing your next sermon, what happens in that time will inform your preaching profoundly. I know one bishop who used to schedule meetings with great theologians. "2pm Tuesday? Sorry, I am meeting with Karl Barth." Someone once suggested to me that it was helpful to "write something in the diary": literally the word "something". It worked for me. Whenever someone wanted me to use that time for another task I would say, "Sorry I've got something in the diary."

Time for Reflection

- ◆ Why do you think Jesus withdrew to pray?
- ◆ What might his ministry have been like if he had not?
- ◆ Have you ever thought when listening to a sermon—your own or someone else's—that maybe it lacks that certain quality which can only come from a certain depth of spirituality? How would you advise such a preacher, maybe yourself, to avoid that kind of superficiality in the future?

Food for Thought

Pain puts time out of joint, but if time is sufficiently out of joint in the first place, great pain may follow.[21]

Why Not . . . ?

Identify two two-hour slots per week in your diary which you can devote to one uninterrupted task? One can be a nurturing task for you, one might be a productive task. If that's not possible try two ninety minute slots—and be more rigorous about not being interrupted and focusing your attention 100%. If ninety minutes is too long go for two one-hour slots . . .

SESSION 15

Threading

There is a whole book to be written about how time is best utilised when the task is to write a book or a very long report. I say "very long" because some people will always say that they are hardwired to leave things to the last minute. There is some truth in this and we will discuss it later. On the other hand, seriously big projects are never done the night before they are delivered, though they might involve a few litres of midnight oil *en route*.

But it's the *en route* that I am talking about here. The threading of a significant amount of work through the diary so that after a few weeks or months something very significant has been achieved. Learning a new skill is always like this. We never start on driving lessons a week before our test. We know that we need time between each learning session to let our new knowledge sink in. As an organist once said to me, time *away* from the console is vital in learning a new piece.

Threading makes sense when you realise that you are involved in a *project* of some kind. One of the subtleties of time wisdom is to recognise and identify projects and to learn how to work at them over an expanse of time.

When they realise that they have more than just a single piece of work on their hands, time-wise people automatically begin to draw together the techniques of clearing and threading. I have certainly used both approaches in preparing this book. Not long after the conference at which I got the idea for something like this I put aside a few afternoons and gave myself the challenge of writing three sessions per sitting. I wrote by hand and as quickly as I could. The product was a bit rough and ready, but it meant that I had a first draft on the table quite quickly and it did not take long, working with a secretary, to create a prototype to try out. Feedback came in and I tinkered with it and developed another version, and put some of it on the web. Other people picked up the resource and began to use it. I got more feedback. Most of this work took place without my needing to set time aside after the initial writing. Then came the opportunity to expand and develop the resource as this book and I found myself making extensive use of clumping, clearing and threading to get the project on to the next stage as a respectable, expanded and enhanced draft.

I am sure this kind of process makes sense and you can see it in the way you work on things that are identified as projects. The time per week spent on the task is far from even and if you just leave it to chance you never get through the most demanding bits and the job never gets done. However, a little judicial clearing, coupled with clumping and followed by some intricate threading are vital tools if you want to make the most of your time and deliver a worthwhile and substantial project.

I have used the example of writing this book but the same thing applies to making a garden, renovating a vintage car, restoring an historic church, or for that matter building a congregation. The difficult thing in ministry is often, I suspect, to be able to identify projects as projects.

The benefits of clearing and threading can come together without the framework of anything that might be called a project. If you can make your cleared time predictable that will be especially good for your application and effectiveness. If you can say, "Every Tuesday afternoon I will keep two hours free for study" you have more chance of doing two hours study per week than if you say, "I will try to find two hours for study every week" or, "I will study when I have some free time". Free time is both a tautology and a myth. Failing to schedule important things is to be responsible for their not being done. "I did not have time" is only very rarely an acceptable excuse. Human beings love predictability, as do all animals. Threading goes with the flow of your genetic hardwiring when it becomes a little routine. It is a time-wise practice.

Time for Reflection

- Can you think of any examples of tasks that are already threaded through your diary?
- Do you see the connection between "threading" and the daily cycle of morning and evening prayer and the annual cycle of the Church's calendar? These are evidence of the deep time wisdom of the Church.

Food for Thought

Basically I view time as not on your side. He'll eat up every minute of your life, and as soon as one has gone he's salivating for the next. It's not a bad thing to remind students of. I never felt like this until I woke up on my 70th birthday, and was stricken at the thought of how much I still wanted to do, and how little time remained.[22]

Why Not . . . ?

The key to threading is to recognise that much more can be achieved over a few months than over a few days or weeks. Go through your diary and identify three bits so work which might be done not only more effectively, but also to a higher standard, by threading them through your diary.

If you are using a threading approach to writing something you will have many drafts. One way to help you do that is to introduce a project timetable and to commit to mini-deadlines. If you can line up one or more person to look at your draft on a certain date you will have created a structure which is likely to deliver and you will gain some valuable feedback. Who can you share project progress with on the three things identified above?

To Work With the Stream of God's Wisdom

If music is the most fundamentally contemplative of the arts, it is *not* because it takes us into the timeless but because it obliges us to rethink time: it is no longer time for action, achievement, dominion and power, not even time for acquiring ideas (you could misinterpret attending to drama or poetry in these terms). It is simply time for feeding upon reality; quite precisely like that patient openness to God that is religious contemplation. [. . .]

A musical event is—whether we know it or not—a moral event, a recovery of the morality of time. We can, of course, ignore this, or even distort it into a soothing interruption of habitual evils. But it retains its unarguable claim: it takes time, it will not be rushed. And it is not less—whether we know it or not—a religious event. It tells us what we are and what we are not, creatures, not gods, creators only when we remember that we are not the Creator, and so are able to manage the labour and attention and expectancy that belongs to art. [. . .]

Each year, the Church renews its understanding of itself and its world in the process, the story, of the Christian year. Above all, in Holy Week and Easter, it takes us inexorably through a series of changing relations, shifting perspectives, that can't be rushed: it leads us through the passion and resurrection of Jesus, which is the centre and the wellspring of what we are. We can't do this with selected highlights, saving time; this is a contemplation, a feeding, that requires our flesh and blood, our patience, our passion. It requires that things are done to us, that we allow ourselves to be changed and enlarged. [. . .]

The authority of music, what silences and holds us, is, then, one of the fullest parables we have of the authority of God; not in commanding and imposing from outside, but in asking for our time, so that it can become a time of mending and building. In that double gift—time given away, time given back—we are taken more deeply into the wisdom of God, and freed from the destructive illusion that *we* are supposed to be God. There is no wisdom for us if we cannot receive it as a gift; because the beginning of wisdom is to know we must come to the reality around us and the reality that sustains us in expectancy, with open hands, not with the lust for domination.

We open ourselves to the gift, yet it doesn't make us passive; it draws out our most strenuous energy. What we learn, in music as in the contemplative faith of which music is a part and also a symbol, is what is it to work *with* the grain of things, to work in the stream of God's wisdom. That is why contemplative faith makes us more not less human, human with the humanity of Jesus, in whom wisdom built a house in our midst; human in patience and expectant attentions, free to give because we have taken time to receive. Our busy ambition and our yearning for control are brought to judgement. The time we wanted to save for our obsessive busyness becomes the time in which grace brings us to our maturity—towards the fullness of Christ's stature and the liberty of God's wisdom.

ROWAN WILLIAMS[23]

PART 5

It's Not about Doing More with Less

This section returns to the subject of prioritising. It cannot be said too often that prioritising is essential not only if we are to survive multiple and overwhelming demands but also if we are to retain our integrity. The person who says that they did not do x, y or z because they did not have time is always saying that it was not as important to them as something else. Prioritising is inevitable. The only question is whether we do it sufficiently and wisely.

> *The basic tool of time management is the "must do" list. The basic tools of time wisdom are the "may do" and "don't do" lists.*

SESSION 16
Stop the Clock

Isn't it strange how you can sometimes forget a whole series of lectures but precisely remember an answer to one question from the audience? The question—to a psychiatrist talking about how to care for people with mental health issues such as depression—was this: "What do you do if you encounter someone who needs about half an hour when you only have five minutes?" The answer? "Make five minutes seem like half an hour".

It sounds odd but it can be done. Indeed, some clergy seem to develop this ability when they step into the pulpit . . . Seriously though, the way to stretch time in pastoral encounters is to go for *intensity of attention*. In other words, when you are in a rush but people need you absolutely there and then, give them 100% attention for a very short period of time. This is far more useful to them, and kind to you, than giving them 50% attention for a longer period.

It is worth thinking about how much or little time we are actually present to others, to the task in hand, or to God. The slightest thing can trigger memories, especially as we get older, and they can be easier to enjoy than the bittersweet delights of the present. The future too can distract us. How many times has some sensitivity been missed in a meeting, service, or pastoral conversation because our attention has passed from the present to the future?

Think about a dartboard. The bull's eye is in the middle, the doubles round the edge and the trebles between a third and half way out from the centre. When you are really paying close attention you are, as it were, hitting the bull's eye. This is great, but you won't be able to keep it up for long. As Daniel Kahneman has written, we correctly talk about "paying attention". Attention is a scarce resource. To pay attention takes real effort. It drains and depletes us. It is much easier to let out minds wander; to let them be vaguely engaged by a variety of variously amusing distractions.

However, the mental image of the dartboard might just help you to remember to focus your attentive skills when doing so will make the present moment deeper and therefore apparently longer.

Imagine you were defusing a bomb. Your attention would be intense and time would be irrelevant. You would, I suggest, be content to be there for as long as it takes. I am not suggesting that pastoral work should be conducted with the intensity of a bomb disposal, but there are times when deep attention can give someone far more than a lengthy visit based on a rambling conversation. There is a place for both, of course, but as the time pressure on ministers grows, so the place for the brief intense clock-stopping encounter is going to get more and more significant within the pastoral repertoire.

To minister well, we must be there "in the moment" with a person or group of people. As we enter the moment, life is enriched and the anxiety and busyness of hurry sickness are eased. Moments of time are always brief, but it is up to us how deep they are. A key aspect of time wisdom is to learn how to pay the amount of attention that any situation or encounter deserves. This is rarely easy and you will never be certain that you have got it quite right. We are in the realm of wisdom here, not scientific calculation. Part of practical wisdom is the capacity to live with uncertainty and responsibility for judgments made on less than full evidence. Generally speaking, however, if you have less time you need to give fuller attention. On the other hand if you attend more fully you need not invest as much time.

Time for Reflection

◆ Think back to a recent pastoral conversation and make a list of all the ways in which your mind wandered.

◆ Think back to a recent meeting and make a list of some of the ways in which the conversation wandered away from the agenda.

Food for Thought

Poetry makes us slow down. It is spare writing, where each word, its rhythm and place in the text, works hard to convey layers of meaning. Often the reader needs to speak the poem out loud. Slow reading is particularly helpful in a society where, increasingly, our electronic communications encourage us to skim read, accept interruption to our concentration, and generally do several things at once rather than ever go deep. Though poetry is deep it can open up our contemplative focus.[24]

Why Not ...?

Ask someone to time the next meeting you run. Literally. With a stopwatch. Record when it actually started, when it moved on from one item to another. You could do the same with a service which maybe feels a little bit lengthy.

SESSION 17
Make Haste Slowly

A number of ministers in training were asked to take part in a project about public speaking. They were told that the task was to give a talk about the Good Samaritan. Before the talk they had to report to a room some way from the lecture theatre. On arrival, half were told that they were in good time and half were told that they were late, and on this basis they were sent off to the lecture theatre a few minutes' walk away. On the way to the lecture the seminarians all encountered a person slumped in an alleyway. The result was that those who thought they were in good time stopped to help, but those who thought they were in a rush did not. Some even stepped over the man to get to their destination on time. And this was to give a talk on the Good Samaritan!

When someone once asked Ludwig Wittgenstein what philosophers should say when they greet one another, he replied, "Take your time".

It is a nice thought and maybe we should take it on board as we seek to minister in a context where hurry sickness is an epidemic and where we both exhibit the symptoms of busyness and allow others to project their own busyness on to us.

"Take your time" should be our implicit message to those whom we encounter in parochial and pastoral work. There is kindness and respect in this, but also pragmatism. The capacity of human beings to slow down when you try to hurry them up is enormous! It is often wise, when dealing with holy matters, whether they are buildings or the heart's affections, to make haste *slowly*.

Time for Reflection

- When was the last time someone said to you, "It's okay, take your time, we can spend as long as it takes"? How did that feel? If no-one has ever said it, say it to yourself—now! How does it feel? No need to rush the answer.
- Does that give you any insight into where the true value of pastoral ministry and church leadership might be found?
- How can you find the capacity to be able to offer the healing gift of time today?

Food for Thought

You can be quite certain that your desire to pray will never interfere with your obligations. It cannot. Your responsibilities are part of you and it is this real, burdened, perhaps even over burdened person, whom God loves and in whom he believes. The temptation always is to think that religion means we must be different, unencumbered by the world. This is not so. Look at the life of Jesus. He lived in a quarrelsome, demanding, hostile world and accepted all of it as the world His father would redeem.[25]

Why Not . . . ?

Have a go at summarising your next sermon as a tweet. That is, try to put your message in 140 characters. It may be impossible but the general idea is that if we put in more thought, effort and prayer our communication becomes briefer and clearer. Memorable messages are always succinct.

SESSION 18
Let Less be More

Time-wise people know the 80:20 rule and let it inform the way they use their time and energy. Also known as the Pareto Principle, the rule says that, on the whole, 80% of the result in any human project, whether a personal or shared enterprise, comes from about 20% of the effort. It is worth dwelling on this both because it is counterintuitive and because it has some radical implications.

It is counterintuitive because we tend to think that, on the whole, 50% of our effort produces 50% of the result, 60% effort creates 60% of the result and it is only with a 100% effort that we will get a 100% result. However, life is not so simple. The sobering, humbling and ultimately liberating reality is that sometimes less effort leads to a better result. This is because often it is only 20% of what we do that really makes the difference. The other 80% is all the other stuff we do alongside the things that really make a difference.

Unfortunately, it is not often possible simply to identify the magical 20% and focus on it. If it were, life would be a lot easier. However, the general principle can help us to be wise about our use of time in all sorts of ways, not least in ministry where all too often we judge our own commitment and care by the amount of time we throw at something.

As Woody Allen once said, "Eighty per cent of success is showing up". We should take this much more seriously in ministry. When we visit people at home or a school or prison, or when we get up to preach, lead prayers or give notices, we need to remind ourselves that much, if not most, of what we say or do is going to make very little difference. It's the 20% that really matters. We should then do and say relatively little, accepting that things like the tone, style, graciousness, humanity and sincerity of what we say count far much more than quantity of time, volume of words, or even amount of effort.

Think about it. When did you last enjoy listening to someone who was too busy to prepare something short and sweet and so went on and on before rushing off to do something else?

The Pareto Principle is obviously not a precise rule, it is a matter of "more or less" 80:20. However, time-wise people know perfectly well that in many things to do with people, less is often more. This is a tough lesson for people in ministry to learn. It is when we stop speaking, when we get up to leave, when we say "over to you" that we not only make room for God's grace, but we also make it clear that we are simply sharing Christ's ministry, not projecting our own ego into a situation.

Time for Reflection

- Could it possibly be true that you talk too much? If so, how can you find ways to talk less in meetings, in pastoral encounters and at church services?
- Is it conceivable that you sometimes overstay your welcome on pastoral visits? Can you find ways of making your engagements and encounters, say, 25% shorter?
- Try out both of the above for a couple of months and then try to be honest about the results. Is your ministry better or worse? Has your time anxiety or busyness abated a little?

Food for Thought

The problem of time is historically central to all religions; indeed, it can be said that one of the main purposes of theological systems has been to provide answers to the menace and mystery of time.[26]

Why Not . . . ?

Put a limit on the number of things you allow to be on your "must do" list.

SESSION 19
Don't Do It!

In the days and weeks after it was announced that I was to leave the parish where I had been rector for twelve years, I had many memorable conversations. One contained this salutatory exchange.

"Do you know that you once did something really wonderful for us?"

"No," I said coyly and began to look forward to hearing what the "wonderful thing" was.

"You went on sabbatical."

I have to admit that I was a bit taken aback by the suggestion that my main contribution had been to get out of the way for a while! But the point was followed up kindly.

"In your first years here things changed so much and we were all a bit dazed. But while you were away we realised that we could keep up the good work without you. That lesson will come into its own now."

It was one of those special, brief conversations that are worth reflecting on deeply. Any illusion that I was indispensable had been shattered. That was good because I was now leaving, but I wonder whether I had been behaving as if I was indispensable for all those years. Maybe I had been doing too much. I know that I worked hard and was often more tired and irritable than I should have been. Like all people who need to get a lot done, I became quite good at time management—which as often as not involves plans and creating and working through to-do lists efficiently.

However, another parish conversation was also important to me. It was with someone else who had a job with impossible expectations. In a brief conversation he told me that every day he had to decide whom he was going to disappoint. It was not that he wanted to disappoint anyone, but that he knew he could not do it all and so felt it was better to do his disappointing intentionally, appreciating, but accepting, the risks involved.

This powerful and strangely wise idea is picked up by leadership guru Tom Peters. "Fact: There's nothing . . . NOTHING . . . easier than writing a 50-item 'TO-DO' list. In which . . . EACH ONE OF THE 50 ITEMS is . . . truly of the Utmost Importance . . ."[27] As Peters goes on to say, it is far more valuable, and difficult, to write a "to don't" list.

This *is* as obvious as it sounds, but much more difficult. It is a list of things that you are under pressure to do but know that, realistically, you are not going to manage.

The advantages of the "to don't" or "don't do" list are enormous. You know whom you are going to disappoint. You save loads of "worry energy" and most importantly you create space to do the most important and difference-making things well. You are less anxious and less busy. Bingo!

The basic tool of time management is the "must do" list. The basic tools of time wisdom are the "may do" and "don't do" lists.

Time for Reflection

- Identify three things that could go on to your first "don't do" list.
- What is the worst that can happen if you really do not do these things?
- Don't do them.

Food for Thought

The time-deniers say: forty's nothing, at fifty you're in your prime, sixty's the new forty, and so on. I know this much: there is objective time, but also subjective time, the kind you wear on the inside of your wrist, next to where the pulse lies. And this personal time, which is the true time, is measured in your relationship to memory. So when this new thing happened—when these new memories suddenly came upon me—it was as if, for that moment, time had been placed in reverse. As if, for that moment, the river ran upstream.[28]

Why Not . . . ?

Write "make a list" as the first item on your "must do" list. That way you get one tick straightaway. Then write something you really want to do on your "may do" list, and be sure to do it.

SESSION 20
A Word in Season

A group of management consultants decided to do some research on leadership. Rather than ask leaders what they did, they observed them closely for a number of months. The results were very interesting. For instance, whereas leaders felt that developing and then disseminating a strategy was the key thing, the observations did not bear this out. The consultants concluded that strategies and presentations (they called them "PowerPoint festivals") are relatively ineffective in making change happen. What matters far more is the right word (or sentence) spoken in the right way *at the right time.*

The suggestion, then, is that real leadership happens *on the hoof and in the moment* and that, rather than try to move things forward by creating strategies, it is more realistic to try to "nudge" things along.[29]

Choosing your moment is a highly developed skill of the time-wise leader. Like so much, it depends on our developing the virtue of patience—but in a grown-up sense. For although patience does mean not rushing things, it should also mean not waiting too long. It is possible to be too patient, too tolerant of people who seek to slow everything down to a standstill.

A new minister in a church facing multiple problems, many of which were unacknowledged by the congregation, was accused of being impatient. The accusation stung because it had been made before. However, after careful reflection the priest came to the conclusion that this "impatience" was actually a gift in this situation because it was, in fact, a crisis.

Time-wise leadership involves discerning matters of urgency. It requires being open to the possibility that, while it would be good to spend a long time building a consensus, action is needed very soon. It also requires the opposite: being open to the possibility that it is anxiety which is causing the panic and that the leader's role is to calm and slow things down.

None of this is easy, but decisions about timing (often made quickly and intuitively) can be among the most important decisions we make.

Time for Reflection

- How do you react to the research about leadership happening "in the moment"?
- How might you best prepare for the unexpected moment when the difference-making word can be spoken? (Hint: it is not by being busy

and anxious.)

Food for Thought

The capacity to be kind to oneself is a mark of wisdom. In the output-driven, activity-focused world of the church today, this is an issue with which many clergy grapple, sometimes paying a high price in mental or physical health.[30]

Why Not . . . ?

Use the phrase, "A word in season, how good it is!" (Proverbs 15.23) as a theme for meditation for the next week or so. Just say it slowly to yourself over and over again. You can do it while sitting quietly in a typically meditative pose, or when walking around, or whenever you have nothing better to think about. Slowly it will sink in and you will realise that the key thing to find is not the right word but the right moment. Discern the moment and the words will flow.

SESSION 21

Taking Advantage of Technology—Without Letting it Take Advantage of You.

One of the facts of modern life is that time-saving devices do not deliver you the gift of more disposable time. We can discuss why until the cows come home. People now have more money than time and lots of people try to sell you ways to save time and to organise yourself better to make the most of what is understood to be a scarce resource.

Some of the things on the market are gimmicks, some suit one person more than another, and some might actually meet your needs perfectly. So here are some things to bear in mind as you consider taking a further step in the gismo-fication of life.

- All new things take time to learn how to use them well. You will have to invest time up front.
- For some of us the new is very exciting and we will want to take the step for the thrill. This might be a good thing. It might not.
- Some gismos can be fascinating and even addictive. A recent report spoke of bishops playing with their BlackBerry smartphones while interviewing clergy for new posts. It happens. Gismos can be like the ring in *The Lord of the Rings*.
- Nothing is going to solve the problem of time. You can squeeze more and more out of the regular 24 hours of a day but you can't make it into a 25 hour day. (The solution to the problem of time is to realise that time is not a problem.)
- Transferring to an electronic diary can be a distraction from the important and urgent matter of sorting out your priorities.
- Given a choice between writing a "to don't list" and playing with an electronic gismo most people would prefer playing. But it is the "to don't list" which will deliver the real results.
- I have recently transferred from a paper diary to using a digital diary synced to my home laptop, my work PC, my PA's PC and my iPad. It's the syncing that makes it possible. I find colour coding different types of activity and putting in recurring slots for things that would otherwise get lost very helpful. It was not a decision I made hastily. I know full well that it's not the device that is time-wise (or not), but me.

Time for Reflection

- Think back over the "time-saving" devices you have purchased and rate them for ease of use, capacity to distract, and success in saving time. What scores best?
- Ask some colleagues to do the same and get them to tell you what their best scoring gadget is.
- There are some things for which pen (or pencil—I prefer pencil) and paper are best—what are they?

Food for Thought

Towards the end of his remarkable book *Thinking, Fast and Slow*, Daniel Kahneman observes that while the mind is "good with stories", it "does not appear to be well designed for the processing of time".[31] This is a very helpful and comforting observation. It's not just me! We all overestimate and underestimate how long things will take. We are all bad at monitoring the passage of time. Human beings are simply not very time-wise. We all need to work at it.

Why Not . . . ?

Spend ten minutes thinking about what you would do with the extra hour if there were 25 in the day after all. Get them into your "may do" column soon.

INTERLUDE
Before the Ending of the Day

How time-wise have you been today? A structured reflection for each day of the week.

Monday:
Have a quick look over your two-column "to do" list.
- How many ticks in the "must" column today?
- How many in the "may" column?
- How happy are you with that (on a scale of 1–5)?

Tuesday:
- Did you at any time give anyone the impression of being "busy"?
- Can you work out why you did that?

Wednesday:
- What was the most time-wise thing you did today?
- If you lived this day again, where would you put in less time?
- What can you add to your "to don't" list?

Thursday:
- What was your most significant interruption today?

Friday:
- Who, or what, was a blessing to you today?

Saturday (or your day off):
- To what extent were you able to switch off to duties today?
- What, if anything, triggered you back into "work mode"?

Sunday:
- How well did you handle the transitions between one moment and the next during the day?

PART 6
Growing Self-Awareness

The following sessions are designed to help you grow in self-awareness and to become a person who inhabits time in your own way. You could say that this bit is about developing your temporal intelligence—a crucial component of time wisdom.

The time-wise approach I am advocating seeks to calm the excess of busyness which is both counterproductive and addictive.

SESSION 22
Watching Your Ps and Js

Some people are larks and some are owls. The larks rise early and find the morning a productive time. The owls do the opposite and flourish at night. Which of these you are will impact the way you work on tasks like sermon preparation, Bible Study or putting together the bid for funding a community project. On the whole, people know what works for them.

There are more subtle cycles than the daily one. All of these have their own energy patterns with peaks and troughs and times which are better for some tasks than others. Time of day, month and year matter, and it is wise to try to fit in with, or maybe make use of, the natural energy that is available.

Knowing your cycles is one aspect of your "time personality" which is an essential dimension of time wisdom. Having a sense of other people's personalities and how their energy waxes and wanes over time is important too. Don't expect close colleagues to be on the same cycle as you.

Another aspect of your time personality has been highlighted by the very well-known personality preference scheme devised by Myers and Briggs and reflecting the psychology of Carl Jung. There are plenty of introductions to the Myers Briggs Personality scheme available in books or on the internet. According to their scheme, each person is characterised by their place on one of four scales. One of the scales is labelled J-P. P types are typically inclined to prevaricate. J types prefer to be in "get on with it", "no-nonsense" mode and high J scorers find anything other than crisp decisiveness very difficult. High Ps on the other hand might find it hard to come to a conclusion or decision.

One of the most successful applications of the Myers Briggs scheme is to help people to understand their colleagues in a close team. In terms of how people work with, and respond to, time the J-P axis is very significant. Faced with a deadline, J types will tend to plan the work and work towards it purposefully, spreading their effort over a planned out programme and maybe completing well ahead of schedule. The P type does not do this. Ps tend to wait until the deadline is almost palpably close before focussing their efforts on the task in hand. Before that they will put in a bit of work, but they will do so erratically.

J preference people enjoy using and maybe even producing time management resources—when, that is, they can see the problem that others have in being organized and getting things done. I myself am a J but not a very high J. I know what it is to dither and be vague (or at least I think I do, not sure, maybe, oh well yes I suppose I do . . .)

Anyway, I come across in work mode as much more J than I am when relaxed or in normal mode—my packing for holidays is very much at the last minute and involves much agonising and rushing around the house looking for I-am-not-sure-what. Even if this is not quite my default, I know that it is a real danger to myself and to others to behave like this when there is serious or significant project on the table. When the work is too big to be done in a final pre-deadline blast, or if other people are put at risk by my prevarication, then I must behave more like a J. That takes us back to the sorts of behaviours we explored earlier: listing, clumping, clearing and threading. If you are P you will have struggled with that stuff, but if you have significant responsibilities you need to be behave like a J—from time to time, at least.

Of course there is flip side to this. Not all work is best dealt with by the planning and decisiveness that come naturally to a J. You could, in our circles, think of P as the pastoral mode. Ps do have time. Ps are able to stay with ambiguity until it becomes clear in its own good time. They have what Keats famously called "negative capability".

I once had the role of leading a rather complex project which involved many levels of negotiation and in the course of which many key stakeholders would inevitably be upset and irritated with me. I did not really appreciate this as I set out, but got the message soon enough (and realised why I had been volunteered for it). Part way through someone said he thought it was going really well and asked me how I was doing it. My answer, on reflection, was that I was using a lot of P. I was standing back from being decisive and letting lots of possibilities open up and then letting the discussion run its course until a kind of misty clarity began to emerge from the dense fog. Later in the project, it was a lot of J that was a called for. And so it is in ministry more generally; think for instance of funeral ministry. At the visit it is the P preference which needs to predominate. In the service itself you need to be J and make sure everything runs to time—especially if you are at a 20-minute slot crematorium and there is someone else waiting to come in behind you. Crematoria are paradise for Js. Ps, on the other hand, would love a graveyard where the grass has not been cut for months.

Time wisdom might involve knowing your Myers Briggs preference type but that is only important if it allows you to be more intentionally flexible and meet the situation with the appropriate decisiveness or openness. What Myers Briggs tells you is what you are going to find easy and what you are going to find difficult.

Time for Reflection

- Are you a lark or an owl?
- How can you organise your life to make the best use of your different energy levels at different times?

Food for Thought

It is one of the fascinations of time that it is both the most intangible of entities and the most inexorable.[32]

Why Not . . . ?

If you haven't already done so, attend a Myers Briggs day so you can find out more about this and see how this aspect of your personality interacts with other parts.

SESSION 23

The Time Paradox

One exercise I have done at parish days recently is to ask people to stand at one end of a hall if they are more at home thinking about the *past*, at the other if they prefer thinking about the *future* and to stand in the middle if they are most comfortable with the *present*. I often add, "If you like to read historical novels go to the past end, science fiction the future, and newspapers or magazines the middle". The result (and remember that this is not scientific!) is that about 40% go to the past end and 40% to the middle—the present. Only 20% go to the future end.

There are two lessons here. First, people do seem to be able to do this. That is, they know whether they prefer past, present or future. Second, many more people prefer the past to the future.

I came up with this exercise after reading the book *The Paradox of Time*[33] which explores the psychology of the perspectives that people have on time. It is of great relevance to anyone in a position of ministerial leadership. For instance, it can help us understand why we get less resistance to pastoral initiatives which involve celebrating the past to bold leadership initiatives which might lead to a new future. Time-wise pastors will know that past, present and future all need to be handled with tact and care and to do that they will need to be comfortable with all three.

You could think of past-oriented people as rowers. They see where they have been. Future-oriented people are canoeists. They look ahead. The present tense folk are perhaps happiest drifting on a raft. It is important to know both who's who, and how many of each you have in your community.

Time for Reflection

- Are you a rower or a canoeist—or do you prefer "now"? How often does parish ministry feel like trying to canoe while others are rowing in the other direction?
- What do rowers think of someone intent on canoeing?
- And what about the mystic on the raft . . . how do they fit into all this?

Food for Thought

Different people experience time differently. They have different "time personalities". As Shakespeare observed in *As You Like It*:

> Time travels in divers paces with divers persons. I'll tell you who Time ambles withal, who Time trots withal, who time gallops withal, and he who stands still withal.

It is wise to recognise this when working in a team or in any collaborative venture. One great place to learn this is when taking holidays with friends. If you are not in some sort of synchrony together life will be a bit tricky now and then—to say the least.

In a team things might be more productive if there is in fact a bit of temporal tension between members. Let those who have a greater sense of urgency pep up the sluggards, and let the patient ones stop the urgent ones rushing headlong into a panic. As leader you might sometimes have to speed things up and other times slow them down.

Why Not . . . ?

This might sound crazy, but . . . why not completely re-organize your papers in an area where you need to freshen up your approach or start out again. The sociologist C. Wright Mills suggests this as integral to a creative process.[34] I myself have found it to be a very powerful technique. Before I could write my book *Healing Agony* I had to reorganise my thoughts on forgiveness. I put more than twenty years worth of work in a heap: my notes, photocopied articles, newspapers cuttings, books, all of it, and simply reorganised it. It took a few hours in several sessions over a few days, but from then on the subject was manageable.

SESSION 24
Time is Not Money

Everybody knows the story of Ebenezer Scrooge. He started off mean and miserable and ended up generous and happy. His humbugging of Christmas turned into the warmest of good wishes. His belligerence became benevolence overnight. Everybody also knows that the difference between "before" and "after" was not a self-determined change of mind, but the terrified response to three ghostly dreams which showed him Christmas past, present and future.

But when everybody knows something you can be sure that everybody has missed something even more obvious and even more important.

A Christmas Carol isn't mainly about miserliness and money. *A Christmas Carol* is about something far more important than money. It is about time.

Ebenezer Scrooge's number one problem was not that he was mean but that he did not have time. Anxious about the pennies, and believing Franklyn's half-truth, "time is money", as if gospel, he gave all his time to his work.

The genius of Dickens, who must have been as industrious as the next man to produce so many words, was that he saw that the fundamental problem was not attitude to money but attitude to time.

There are plenty of witty clues in the book itself to suggest that time is the true theme of *A Christmas Carol*. The three ghosts at the heart of the story ("past", "present" and "future") have the task of introducing our anti-hero to the temporal dimension. Their visits come at precisely one o'clock in the morning and, while they are all extensive, they take no time. A main focus of Scrooge's bullying of Bob Cratchit was timekeeping. Towards the end of the book the new Scrooge gets to work early so that he can catch Bob coming in late. Dickens uses the drama of the ticking clock to bring it vividly to life. "The clock struck nine. No Bob. A quarter past. No Bob. He was a full eighteen and a half minutes, behind his time." As the book ends there is a new hint every minute for the reader. "It's only *once a year*, sir", pleads the tardy Bob. "I was making rather merry *yesterday,* sir."

It all becomes brilliantly clear as Scrooge's conversion to a better life is narrated. Certainly he vows to honour Christmas in his heart. The next step is to try to keep it all year. We are getting close now, but are not yet at the nub of the matter. But here it comes: Scrooge declares, "I will live in the Past, the Present and the Future. The Spirits of all Three shall strive within me. I will not shut out the lessons that they teach."

What Scrooge learnt is that time is *not* money. It is far more subtle and significant than that. It is in the 3D quality of the moment, the richness of the whole life, that true wealth is to be found.

The lesson of *A Christmas Carol* is this: rather than being money, time is priceless.

Time for Reflection

+ List three ways in which time *is* like money.
+ List three ways in which time *is not* like money.

Food for Thought

It is said that the composer Leonard Bernstein used to remark that in order to achieve great things you needed to have a plan and "not quite enough time".

Time pressure can be a good thing. It can get the juices going. It can get people to step the effort level up a bit. But like many good things there is an optimal amount. A little is good but too much is bad. Nonetheless, a little bit of rush, a tiny bit of haste, an occasional "let's get on with this", maybe even a soupçon of impatience, might sometimes be just what is needed.

Why Not . . . ?

Exercise a "no talking that is not essential to running the meeting" rule on yourself next time you are chairing a meeting. Afterwards, reflect on what you learnt.

SESSION 25

Procrastination

I have on my desk a very unlikely spiral bound dairy called *Do it Later! A 2012 Planner (or Non-Planner) for the Creative Procrastinator*. It's just the sort of thing for people who hate the advice of "holier-than-thou time-management gurus" (a phrase I discovered in *Do It Later!*). Every double page spread has one page for the days of the week and another which is essentially a to-do list with subheads. Here are the subheadings:

- Things I have to do but can wait a day or two or three . . .
- Small things I have to do before I can do the big things I have to do.
- Things I absolutely have to do unless I absolutely don't want to do them.
- Things people have been bugging me to do for a really long time.

And at the top of every such page there is a sentence of "procrastinator wisdom". For instance:

- "If it comes to mind, do it. If not, don't."
- "Checking your email and visiting your homepage every ten minutes makes you a very informed person."
- "No ifs and buts about it: one day I might stop procrastinating."
- "To work is noble, to procrastinate divine."

It's a great diary—or anti-diary—and it spells out exactly the complex of ideas and attitudes that is at the heart of procrastination in an amusing and ironic way. Reading it, I am not sure whether it is seriously meant as a two finger salute to time management or whether it is a clever reverse psychology attempt to help those who really can't put off the habit of putting things off. It is this ambiguity that it has prevented me giving *Do it Later* to any of my friends or colleagues. I don't want to provoke the question, "Who are *you* calling a procrastinator?" Either that or it is because I just haven't got round to it yet.

If you look up the definition of the verb "procrastinate" it simply means to delay or defer an action until later. Looked at from a straightforward time management perspective, this is a great sin. You have assigned this task to this time—you must do it. A time wisdom perspective sees procrastination differently. Time wisdom recognises both the importance of doing what you plan to do and recognising that sometimes other things crop up. A time management manual gives the example: you had planned to spend a day clearing out your garage and the roof is leaking—you procrastinate on the garage task and get the roof done. Well, that's obvious and easy. The water is coming in! Ministry and leadership sets up many much more trying puzzles and problems for us: "Do I do this as I had planned or respond to that which has just come to my attention?"

It is this ongoing decision-making which is the most demanding aspect of practical time wisdom, and the reason I have kept this session near to the end is to suggest that we can only handle the procrastination dilemmas well when we have established a solid foundation of time wisdom.

My contention is this: if you have got beyond the busyness syndrome and are working with the basic tools of clearing, chunking, listing and so on, and if you have a background sense of time and its meaning for you, then you will be in the best possible position to respond positively to the unforeseen and unplanned and to prioritize it over planned tasks.

In fact, I would say that it is a mark of mature and good ministry to be an expert and skilled procrastinator at the same time as exercising good and clear leadership.

Procrastination can be negative of course: it is all too easy to engage in "displacement activities" when the main task makes us anxious or bored. It is easier to tweet a joke than think hard enough to be able to produce a really good and simple sermon. It is more congenial to stay chatting with a nice person you have just bumped into than make that difficult phone call. It is a piece of cake to delude yourself that you will do tomorrow what you do not find in the least attractive today. And the result of such self-indulgent procrastination is that before too long you find yourself living in that "tomorrow" where too many things have become urgent and you are having to deal with all the consequences of not having put in ten minutes of fire-prevention work in the past.

Time for Reflection

- If there were a Procrastination Quotient (PQ rather than IQ or EQ) what would your score be? (100 is the average and 150 is genius level.)
- What would a meeting of the PQ equivalent of Mensa be like?

Food for Thought

In a beautiful book simply called *The Sabbath*, Rabbi Heshel says that Judaism is a religion of time. He makes the point that human beings are all "infatuated with the splendour of space" and that it is our deep desire to control it. But, he argues, we fail to understand or appreciate time. We seek to use it to help us master space. We treat it as tool but are not able to face it on its own terms. This creates an imperative to work out our relationship with time; a relationship which itself informs and qualifies our relationship with space.

For Herschel, then, the Sabbath is a cathedral or a temple of time. He also calls it a palace. It is splendid, spacious beautiful and holy time. "The meaning of the Sabbath", he says, "is to celebrate time rather than space."[35]

Why Not . . . ?

Cut through some of the muddle and confusion that is going on at the moment by admitting a mistake and apologising. It short circuits a lot of the gossip and undermines the corrosive backward-looking analysis which is involved in finding out how much blame each person deserves. Take the lot and throw it away.

SESSION 26
Punctuality

By now you should have been cured of hurry sickness and feel able to live and work at a sensible pace, knowing that while you will never get everything done you will get the things done that matter most and that you will achieve far more over the coming year by not being busy than by being busy.

So the old Rev. Rush, whom you perhaps were, is no more.

But it is possible that you are still the *late* Rev. Rush in the sense that you are never on time. Chronic tardiness is a condition which comes naturally to some people, just as chronic and rather annoying earliness comes to others. Neither is wise; neither is healthy. If your growing time wisdom has not dealt with your habit of lateness it might be worth thinking through why this is. Once you have analysed it, finding a way of changing your behaviour will be relatively straightforward. Take a deep breath and try this exercise.

I am chronically late because:

1. I sleep too much and am behind schedule from the moment I get going in the morning.
2. I don't worry about keeping other people waiting—their time is less important than mine.
3. I simply underestimate how long it will take to get from A to B.
4. I always try to do one last thing before I leave for the next appointment.
5. I spend a lot of time looking for keys etc. when I should be on my way.
6. I haven't got the skill or courage to say to people that I must now leave their company and go on to the next thing.
7. It's just my personality and there is nothing to be done about it.

If you are anything like me, you will be able to tick more than one box—my prevailing sin is 4. But I also suffer from 5, 6 and sometimes 3.

Here are some thoughts about how you might overcome these various causes of tardiness:

1. Sorry to be blunt, but you either have to get up earlier or do some more work on that "to don't" list. I know which I prefer.
2. Thank you for being honest. But honesty does not cover up the sin of arrogance. You need to change your attitude.

3. Help is at hand. A zillion gadgets are queuing up to tell you how long your journey should take. And please be honest. Many people have often been late for a meeting who would never be late for a party or to catch the plane to go on holiday.

4. As I said, this is me. It's to do with being too locked into the moment, too much in the flow of what you are doing. I have often kicked myself (metaphorically) when driving or rushing to something needlessly late because once on my journey I realised that the task that had delayed me was not really urgent at all.

5. This happens to me too. Predictably enough, it is more likely when I am already rushing because of having tried to do one or two last minute tasks. It is, however, a very good idea to have your bag packed and ready to pick up well before you go. That way you might just get away with squeezing in an extra task or two.

6. I know about this one too. Partly it is assertiveness. Partly it is not wanting to be rude. Partly it is pastoral. People start to open up just as it is time for you to leave. Partly it is poor planning. You have scheduled these things too closely. The answer, I expect is to find a way to clarify when you will need to leave as the meeting begins. It's more difficult in a pastoral situation, but it is possible. It will only be rude if you have not actually arrived early enough to give the people the time they need.

7. Well I've heard that one before. To be honest I don't buy it. Certainly some personality types find being on time more difficult than others. However, there are questions of character here too. My hunch, cynic that I am, is that this is an excuse to cover your tracks if you really think and feel "2".

Time for Reflection

◆   Write an email to yourself (and please do send it) explaining how you feel when other people are late for things which matter to you.

◆   Can you tell people why there is no evidence whatsoever that starting things late is an effective use of time? (At the same time as recognising that sometimes there will be a legitimate reason for doing so.)

Food for Thought

The wisdom of time is knowing what each moment is for, discerning at any given time the nature of the opportunity that lies before us.[36]

Why Not . . . ?

Make that "don't do" list.

SESSION 27
Planning

Planning is a highly controversial and complex subject. Think of the rows that can happen over planning applications in the local community and the sterility which can occur in politics or business when everything is reduced to a dreaded "five-year plan". There is a lot to be said *against* planning, as those who are involved in the reality of pastoral ministry know only too well.

"The best laid plans o' mice an' men / oft gang agley" wrote Robert Burns in his *Ode to a Mouse*. The scenario is familiar. You spend some quality time planning your day, settle down to work through your list and the phone rings. It's the Funeral Director or the Churchwarden and the plan or "must do" list goes out of the window.

There is some truth in that, but not the whole truth. Planning has got a bad name because it is often seen as a more precise or determinative science than it ever really can be. But the fact that Plan A never quite works out does not mean that Plan A is useless or that it has been a "waste of time" to prepare it. On the contrary, the point about Plan A is that it is a tool that puts you in the best position to cope with the unexpected. As someone has put it, "Planning is priceless, plans are useless."

Planning the day, the week, the month, the year ought to be a priority for any time-wise person. It's the best way to begin to get a grip on time anxiety and busyness. However, we must always remember that our plans and to-do lists are provisional and if we are wise we will always include "respond to the unexpected" on our to-do list and some "catch-up" time in our diary or calendar.

Time for Reflection

- Are there areas of your ministry where more planning and less "spontaneity" (often "reaction") would be positive?
- Can you think of a time when you actually coped better with the unexpected because you had a plan which was never actually delivered?

Food for Thought

No one enjoys waiting. It is when we wait that time feels heavy and slow. When we are waiting we feel frustrated. We lose whatever delights and opportunities the present moment might have and experience a strange tension—the tension born of the fact that the future has not yet arrived.

In his book *The Stature of Waiting*, W.H. Vanstone makes the point that "Any kind of waiting presupposes some kind of caring. One cannot be said to wait for something that is a matter of indifference."[37] He goes on to argue that a person who really cares will not be a stranger to waiting. If we really care, we have to learn how to wait.

Waiting need not be a matter of passivity—any more than listening or looking is passive. Waiting is the recognition that the right time is not yet. There is humility in waiting because it recognises that the right time is not something we can control.

Learning how to wait is part of time wisdom. It is the recognition that time that matters cannot be managed.

Why Not . . . ?

Spend fifteen minutes sketching out what might be possible in three years' time. Only one rule: think of at least three people who will instantly dismiss what you are planning as "impossible".

SESSION 28

URGENT (and not-so-urgent)

I once worked with someone who always sought to get my attention by using the word "URGENT"—and yes, in capital letters. After a while I realised that they were just trying to jump the queue and it was distracting me from matters that were important or strategic. The relationship did not end as happily as one would hope. The lesson that I took from it was to try never to use the urgent word, and if I did use it then to do so apologetically. "I am sorry but this has become urgent", or, "To my surprise this new issue has sprung up and I need to draw it to your attention." The word "urgent" does have meaning but it is a goal of time wisdom to make its use unusual.

Time management gurus (whether holier-than-thou or not) often distinguish between urgent and important. They are right to suggest that people confuse the two. It is also the case that people who suffer from hurry sickness or busyness syndrome tend to make the mistake of confusing them more than others. I once used the idea of "flashing-blue-light ministry" to describe what I felt I was observing in the way some colleagues responded to pastoral need. There was a lot of bother and rush and, if I am honest, some ministerial competitiveness going on. Who would be first on the scene when someone's illness took a turn for the worse? How quickly could you get to a hospital bedside? How soon with a family after a death, or could you be there "just in time" to offer prayers before a final breath?

There is something to be said for such ministry. The feedback is often good and a saintly glow begins to be associated with the minister in a rush. But it has many downsides, as people discover over the years: the ego begins to enjoy the praise and the adrenalin rush a bit too much, while others tend to sit back with their feet up. Family and friends tend to be disempowered or put into second place in their caring and support ("The vicar's here now!"). It is the sort of ministry which grows ministerial egos more than it grows congregations. Now I do believe that ministers need to have egos and to be able to feel a good pride in what they do, but that pride should come as much from seeing others grow in discipleship and ministry as it does in realising that they themselves can make a difference and can be a real channel of grace. The time-wise approach I am advocating does not deny that. What it seeks to calm down is the excess of busyness which is both counterproductive and addictive, and for which ministerial families often pay the price.

As well as distinguishing between urgent and important, time management books often suggest creating a table as shown in Figure 5.

	IMPORTANT	NOT IMPORTANT
URGENT		
NON-URGENT		

Figure 5: Urgency vs Importance

The idea is that such a table helps you organise your "must do" list—whether that is an actual written list or a load of items buzzing round in your mind. To be honest I can't recall any occasions when I have actually drawn this table and allocated things to it, but it is definitely part of my mental furniture. Just having it in your mind and knowing that something can be urgent and not important or important but not urgent is very liberating (especially if someone is sending you messages marked URGENT.)

I can see that perhaps there have been occasions when I might have used such a table when working with colleagues in a team. Maybe at the beginning of a meeting to say, "Okay, of all the items on your mind, let's put them in one of the boxes on the table and then lets divide our time between the important and urgent and the important and not urgent." "But what about the urgent but not important?" someone would ask. The team would then have to think: if it is not important then why be distracted by it . . .

One time wisdom trick I often use is to put things that are both urgent and important to the bottom of my list. This sounds a little bit naughty, but the logic of it goes like this: if it is urgent and important I am going to make sure that I do it today come hell or high water. It is also likely that there will be something of a buzz about it. Furthermore if I know I have to do it today, but try to do something else before (which is maybe a little dull or even a bit tricky or difficult) then I can use a bit of the pressure and adrenalin from knowing that I have an urgent task to do later to push me on with the dull or difficult task which I will do first.

I called it a trick but maybe it is a skill. Certainly you can get it wrong and leave the urgent thing too late. That's no good, but it is also not good if you put your best energy into an urgent task after urgent task so that you never put any real energy into non-urgent but important tasks. Such tasks include any strategic planning for complex events or projects in the future, subtle and sensitive pastoral or HR work. Also, if your ministry is dominated by the concept of "urgent", you can probably say goodbye to any prospect of spiritual depth or theological profundity.

Yes, there are times when you must "drop everything and run", but they are fewer and farther between than we often appreciate.

One Christmas morning, when I was chaplain of King's College, Cambridge, someone came up to me with a look of panic and urgency and said, "There is water coming through the roof." There were about 1,000 people in the building and I was taking the service as well as organising the extra clergy brought in for the occasion to help with the distribution of communion. I looked at the person and looked up at the roof. "It's a long way up there," I said and simply got on with what I was doing. Of course the roof needed to be fixed, but not then. A few years later the flat roof over the sitting room on the vicarage where I was living began to leak profusely—again on Christmas day, but this time in the afternoon. On this occasion it was right to interrupt what was ongoing and planned and sort it out—and discover to my shame that the problem had been caused by my neglect of the routine work of clearing leaves from gutters over the weeks of the autumn.

Time for Reflection

- How do people in your church or wider context try to grab your attention and make themselves, or their agenda, your priority? If they all have the same trick then maybe there is something about you they are hooking into? Do you actually enjoy "flashing-blue-light ministry" more than the steady plod of everyday effectiveness?
- Can you remember any times when you dropped everything and ran only to find that what you were attending to was less important than what you had dropped? How are you going to make sure that doesn't happen very often while remaining open and responsive?

Food for Thought

The Christian faith, above all because of its commitment to the Son's assumption of creaturely reality (including time) in Jesus Christ and the Spirit's direction of all temporal things to their eschatological fulfilment, announces that our experience of temporality corresponds to a dimension of created reality, conferred by the Creator. Music, I have tried to argue, entails practices in which time is experienced not as an inert container (or merely as a human construct) but as an intrinsic dimension of physical entities and events. More than this, the Christian faith affirms that this temporality is a gift, and that consequently it is neither neutral nor inherently threatening. Consequently our interaction with temporality need not be characterised by struggle, competition, intrusion or invasion; nor need it be marked by retreat, evasion or escape. Music . . . can provide a concrete means of establishing and experiencing more contented "living peaceably" with time than our contemporary existence seems able to offer.[38]

Why Not . . . ?

Decide never to use the word "urgent" again.

Developing a Timescape

In my contribution to the book *Developing Faithful Ministers,* I introduced the idea of "timescape". It was my attempt to nuance the idea of "Rule of Life" in a way which does justice to the insights, as I understand them, of a "time wisdom" rather than a "time management" approach. Many things that apply to a Rule of Life might apply to a timescape, but a timescape is less of a set of directions and more a living, breathing, evolving map of the *territory* of time. The analogy is, of course, with landscape. Just as a landscape can seem to be entirely objective, a given of nature, it rarely is. Any landscape will have human features, whether they are architectural or to do with the way crops are planted or animals husbanded. The artist Rigby Graham always includes a dark human element in his landscapes. Some bit of junk or a ruin or some evidence of human spoiling or pollution. It is salutary warning against too romantic a view of nature. Landscape is rarely untouched by some thought, desire, application or intervention. The same is true of timescape. Certainly time has objectivity. It *is* today today, so to speak, and it is possible to be late for an appointment. Deadlines are real. It is a mistake, however, to overestimate the objectivity of time and to underestimate the role which we have as individuals and cultures in shaping our own experience of it.

In 2008 the inventor John Taylor made a clock for Corpus Christi College, Cambridge, in honour of the clockmaker John Harrison who became famous in the book and film *Longitude.* The clock has three features which help to break down the illusion that time is merely objective. The first, and most prominent, is the large grasshopper-like insect which sits on top of the clock. Taylor calls this a *chronophage* or "time eater". As time goes by it opens and closes its mouth, seeming to eating up the passing seconds. It also winks from time to time, apparently expressing a kind of satisfaction in consuming time. The second feature is the way in which the clock marks the hour. It does not strike a bell or chime. Rather, a sound is made by a chain dropping into a small wooden coffin hidden behind the face of the clock. Thirdly, the clock is only accurate every five minutes. Between times it speeds up and slows down, expressing the relativity of time—an experience we all know but which clocks (other than Taylor's) never reveal.

The Corpus Clock is unusual, if not unique, in drawing our attention to these subjective subtleties of time. A timescape must be equally subtle, not making the assumption that time is a rigid, cold, objective reality but accepting its relational, relative and subjective qualities. A timescape is a temporal environment which is inhabited and lived intentionally and with authenticity. Getting this right—and we will never get it *quite* right—is integral both to our holiness as people and our effectiveness as ministers.

What, then, are the contours of a good and liveable timescape? In the previously-mentioned essay I suggest that there are three important qualities: a connection with the wider timescape of the Church; realism about your stage in life, and both your needs and the needs of your dependents; and a firm but flexible quality, an elasticity that will allow it to be stretched when necessary.

Monastic life in the tradition of St Benedict is based on a rigorous observation of the "hours" of prayer. Clocks and bells are important in monasteries, as they are in all institutions where many people need to be doing the same thing at the same time—schools are the most obvious example, though the noise which used to greet the ringing of the school bell back in my day was anything but monastic. Over the years I have grudgingly become convinced about the wisdom of the timetable. Timetables enshrine and apply the principle that things should stop when the time runs out rather than when the work comes to its natural break. It is both frustrating and efficient. It also goes with the grain of the human psyche which likes predictability. Virtues are, essentially, our better habits, and it is remarkable how effective you can be when you rely on a habitual way of working. To give a personal example, until working on this project I had never been very successful at creating or using "to do" lists. The two column "must do" and "may do" list idea gave me encouragement to have a final attempt. After a few weeks of this effortful persistence I began to find the task of drawing up the list becoming easier. It is now part of my routine at the start of the day. I open the clipboard file, add a new piece of scrap paper, write the date, draw the two columns, transfer the undone items from yesterday and write down a few more things in the "must do" column and a couple of things I'd rather like to do in the "may do" column. All it takes is just a few minutes, after which the day feels much more manageable, partly because I know it will be lived not only more effectively but also more gracefully. With the list in place I will know how to deal with surprises and interruptions. I will have some idea of the consequences of not ticking certain things off, if that is what happens—it usually is.

The two column to-do list has therefore become part of my daily routine and an important aspect of my timescape. But it is more than that; it is a something like a set of spectacles through which to see the time, the minutes and hours, of the coming day.

A calendar is a similar thing for longer periods of time. A time-wise person will often look at their calendar to see the patterns and, if there are none, bring some order to it though techniques like clumping and threading. For those in ministry, the great festivals bring special privileges, delights and demands. It is odd, though, to see clergy who seem to be surprised that Christmas is coming soon or that Holy Week is arriving before adequate preparation has been possible. If this happens to you it means that your timescape is a bit distorted. Staring at a calendar in disbelief on Palm Sunday might not sort that out but talking with someone else while staring at their calendar and yours could be a way to create a more helpful map of the temporal territory.

Flexibility is an important aspect of our personal timescape. We should not expect it to be the same over the years. If you share your home with young children then you face very different demands than those whose children have left home. Similarly, if you have elderly relatives in a different part of the country you will need to develop patterns of engagement and connection which allow you to be obedient to the fifth commandment ("Honour your father and mother").

Mention of the Ten Commandments raises the question of the sabbath. In the New Testament we can see that the inherited timescape is challenged by the teaching for Jesus, while the subject is all but ignored by Paul. The sabbath commandment does not feature in Jesus' list of commandments in Matthew (19.17–20) or in Paul's in Romans (13.8–10). Paul's interest in that passage is much more on "now". "Besides this, you know what time it is, how it is now the moment for you to wake from sleep . . . the night is far gone, the day is near" (Romans 13.11, 12). And one of Jesus' better known sayings it that, "The sabbath was made of humankind, not humankind for the sabbath" (Mark 2.27). It is, I suggest, unhelpful to see this as Jesus changing the rules. It is more to do with Jesus introducing a more subjective and relative understanding of time, a different timescape. It does not add up to meaning that Jesus had no time for time, or for regulating things with regard to time or using time as a practical means of collaboration and community. It does mean that he was suggesting a more sophisticated connection between spirituality, salvation and time than had previously been adopted or experienced. It is important that this more subtle and compassionate approach to the relationship between human beings and time, and in particular to the rules, regulations and expectations regarding time is reflected in the way we inhabit time in ministry. This does not mean we can be happily late for appointments but it does mean that we need to be creative, compassionate and intelligent in the way in which we not only view our timescape but also inhabit it.

A good timescape will, of course, allow for different types of time; for time dedicated to different activities and pursuits. Many speak, rather strangely to my ears, of the need for a work-life balance. It is strange because it suggests that life begins when work stops. This is a serious category error for anyone with a sense of vocation, but it does flag up the important question of the needs of human beings for relaxation, recreation and the friendly unfocussed association that is fellowship and family life. For people with limited leisure— and that is everyone who has got as far as reading this—these things need to be crafted into the timescape. Quite how that is done is a matter for personal discernment given the many other features which make your own timescape so interesting. But it is likely that a good timescape will have the organic and ecological feel of a landscape which, while unlikely to be free of human shaping, does have a natural look to it and is both attractive and sustainable. No one wants their timescape to look like a grid or a list and it is important that all the tools for time management that a time-wise person employs are secondary to the bigger issues like overall purpose, wholeness of life, integrity, spirituality, fellowship and personal and social responsibility.

What this suggests, then, is an approach to time which avoids the Scylla of the distressing, unproductive and unsustainable mania of *busyness* and the Charybdis of the dull and enervating programming of life which comes from an overzealous approach to *controlling* oneself and others either through religious or social tradition or through the application of the techniques of time management. Time wisdom is the virtue which finds the middle way not as a narrow path but as a broad and attractive timescape which each person helps to construct and then navigates while achieving multiple objectives in ways which are consistent with their personal values, priorities and convictions; in a word, their *faith*.

Acknowledgements

This book is a product of my work with many colleagues in the diocese of Durham over the last six years. I am especially grateful to those who attended the Clergy Summer Gathering on "Time Matters" back in 2009 for their participation and enthusiasm. It was this brief conference that allowed me to begin to make the broader range of connections which have come together here. I am also grateful to all those who used and gave me feedback on my experimental booklets about "Time Wisdom" and for the two focus groups that spent time with me discussing these matters. One was of experienced incumbents, the other of curates. Both were very helpful to the development of the project. After that some offered feedback on the developing text and I am especially grateful to David Chadwick, Matt Tarling and Sheila Williamson for their written comments.

I am not sure that these ideas would have ever come to light in this format had I not been invited to contribute a chapter on "Time Wisdom" to *Developing Faithful Ministers* and I am grateful to Tim Ling and Lesley Bently for their invitation to be involved in that, and to my fellow authors for their response to my draft which convinced me that there was more to say than could be said in one chapter.

Finally, it has been great to work with Richard and Thomas at Sacristy Press and to develop with them what I hope proves to be an accessible and helpful resource for many.

Endnotes

1. Theodore Roosevelt, from a speech printed in the *Kansas City Star*, 1st November 1917.

2. This was subsequently published; see N.T. Wright, "Case Study: Sabbath", in *Scripture and the Authority of God* (SPCK, 2011)

3. Barbara Adam, *Time* (Polity Press, 2004), p. 3

4. Alec Mackenzie and Pat Nickerson, *The Time Trap* (Amacom, 2009)

5. Ann McGee-Cooper, *Time Management for Unmanageable People* (Bantam Books, 1994)

6. From a report on time spent on a clergy exchange with the Diocese of Alba Iulia in Romania, by The Revd Rupert Kalus.

7. Ann McGee-Cooper, *Time Management for Unmanageable People* (Bantam Books, 1994), p. 11

8. Eugene H. Peterson, *The Contemplative Pastor: Returning to the Art of Spiritual Direction* (Eerdmanns, 1989), p. 17

9. Luke 12.22–31

10. "Diaryoploly" is the name I have given to the game clergy unthinkingly, but competitively, play when trying to fix a meeting date and they all tell each other what is in their diaries when various dates are suggests. I describe it more fully and discuss its toxic consequences in my in my chapter in *Developing Faithful Ministers: A Practical and Theological Handbook*, Tim Ling and Lesley Bentley (eds.) (SCM, 2012), pp. 97–107.

11. Timothy Radcliffe OP, *Why Go to Church: the Drama of the Eucharist* (Continuum, 2008), p. 40

12. Owen Chadwick, *Michael Ramsey: A Life* (SCM, 1990), p. 361

13. St Augustine, *Confessions* (4th cent.), ch. 11, sec. 14

14. Philip G. Zimbardo and John Boyd, *The Time Paradox: The New Psychology of Time That Will Change Your Life* (Free Press, 2008), p. 43

15. Samuel Wells, *God's Companions: Reimagining Christian Ethics* (Blackwells, 2006), p. 2

16. To be fair to those who advocate time management, there are lots of interesting ways to do this. It need not be a matter of crossing most of them out. You could write each one on a piece of paper or card and put them in different piles. Or do the same with post-its. Or divide them in two and put half away for next week. All these ideas are worth trying. My point is simply that some

people will find it much easier than others and that for some the more they get into this the worse it will all get until all attempts to manage time are seen as "a complete waste of time" and we are all back at square one.

17. I have adopted this idea from Alec Mackenzie and Pat Nickerson, *The Time Trap*, 4th edn. (Amacom, 2009).

18. Hugh Rayment-Pickard, *The Myths of Time: From St. Augustine to American Beauty* (DLT, 2004), p. 89

19. Daniel Kahneman, *Thinking, Fast and Slow* (Allen Lane, 2011)

20. Psalm 39.4–6

21. Eva Hoffman, *Time* (Profile Books, 2009), p. 103

22. John Taylor, inventor of the Corpus Clock in *The Guardian*, 18th September 2008. Reprinted by permission.

23. Rowan Williams, "Keeping Time", in *Open to Judgement: Sermons and Addresses* (DLT, 1994), pp. 247–250

24. Janet Morely, *The Heart's Time* (SPCK, 2011), p. ix. Reprinted by permission of SPCK.

25. Sr Wendy Beckett, *Sister Wendy On Prayer* (Continuum, 2006), pp. 21, 22

26. Eva Hoffman, *Time* (Profile Books, 2009), p. 163

27. Thomas J. Peters, *Leadership* (Dorling Kindersley, 2005), p. 56

28. Julian Barnes, *The Sense of an Ending* (Jonathan Cape, 2011), p. 122. Reprinted by permission of The Random House Group Limited.

29. For more on this see George Binney et al., *Living Leadership: A Practical Guide for Ordinary Heroes*, 1st edn. (Pearson Education, 2005).

30. Michael Sadgrove, *Wisdom and Ministry: The Call to Leadership* (SPCK, 2008), p. 92. Reprinted by permission of SPCK.

31. Daniel Kahneman, *Thinking, Fast and Slow* (Allen Lane, 2011), p. 407

32. Eva Hoffman, *Time* (Profile Books, 2009), p. 14

33. Philip G. Zimbardo and John Boyd, *The Time Paradox: The New Psychology of Time That Will Change Your Life* (Free Press, 2008)

34. C. Wright Mills, "On Intellectual Craftsmanship", in *The Sociological Imagination* (Penguin, 1970)

35. Abraham Joshua Heschel, *The Sabbath* (Shambhala Publications, 1951)

36. Hugh Rayment-Pickard, *The Myths of Time: From St. Augustine to American Beauty* (DLT, 2004), p. 90

37. W.H. Vanstone, *The Stature of Waiting* (DLT, 1982), p. 102

38. Jeremy S. Begbie, *Theology, Music and Time* (CUP, 2000), p. 97

Lightning Source UK Ltd.
Milton Keynes UK
UKOW041354050213

205859UK00007B/219/P